Endorsem

Uplift: A Pilot's Journey is a must rea
informational and educational, it describ
a goal, a dream and a burning desire to become an airline pilot. An aviation background is not a necessity in order to understand this author.
Grant Corriveau exhibits a natural talent whether he is talking about
some of the challenges along his journey or major turning points in his
career. He describes things in a simple manner that enables you to picture the message he is trying to convey in your mind's eye.

Grant's book makes one thing very clear. Although the journey has
its challenges and sacrifices, the rewards far outweigh the disadvan-
tages. There is nothing more amazing than peering out the window
over the nose of an aircraft to view what Mother Nature has painted
on the canvas of the earth and sky.

Like Grant, I am an airline pilot. I have to congratulate him for his
dedication and perseverance. Writing a book is no easy task. I feel
fortunate to have Grant not only as a fellow pilot but as a friend. His
accomplishments are an inspiration to both current and future pilots.

— Brian Zetts, Dash 8 Captain (retired), Air Atlantic

If you want to get a feel for what it's like to be an airline pilot, what
it takes to get there and what to expect along the path to becoming a
professional pilot, read this book. *Uplift* is the best investment you'll
have made in preparation for your career in aviation. I love the book!
I could not put it down while reading it, thoroughly enjoyed it and wish
Grant total and complete success with it.

— Salvatore Di Trapani, A320 Captain, Jet Blue

Grant has written an entertaining memoir of an aviation career filled
with many ups and downs, both at his job and in life. You will enjoy
the short anecdotes and various experiences of one airline pilot with a
good sense of humor. It's a great read and I'm sure you will enjoy it.

— Jim Runyon, Captain, Air Canada (retired)

UPLIFT

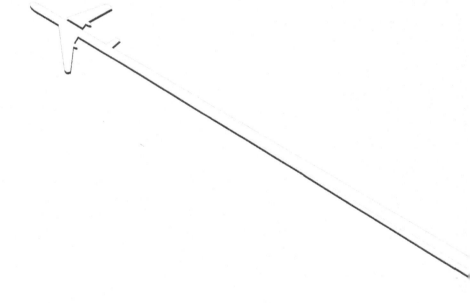

CORRIVEAU

UPLIFT: A Pilot's Journey
by Grant M. Corriveau

Copyright © 2018 CWRpress

Cataloging-in-Publication Data

Corriveau, Grant M., 1949 -
Uplift: A Pilot's Journey / Grant M. Corriveau

Includes biographical references and glossary.

ISBN-978-1-98-7762983   1-98-7762983

1. Autobiographical—Memoir
2. Aviation
I. Title

Author's Disclaimer

These stories are based on true events, as imperfectly as I recall them. Names have been changed to protect the privacy of others. Some characters are composite stand-ins, representing several individuals. Events and conversations may be altered for literary effect.

Italicized bold text has been used herein to indicate the first mention of aviation terms found in the glossary.

Published by CWRpress, Pasadena, CA
info@ptm.org

UPLIFT

A Pilot's Journey

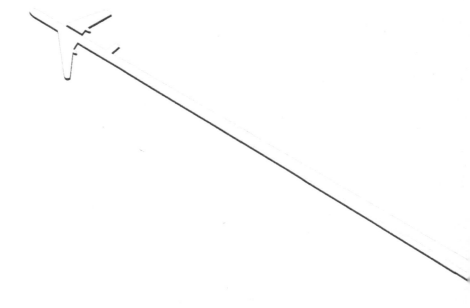

Grant M. Corriveau

CWR Press

To France, Paul and Terri
who have shared so much of this journey with me.
You've made it even more amazing.
Thanks.

Flying Crooked

The butterfly, the cabbage white,
(His honest idiocy of flight)
Will never now, it is too late,
Master the art of flying straight,

Yet has—who knows so well as I?—
A just sense of how not to fly:
He lurches here and here by guess
And God and hope and hopelessness.
Even the aerobatic swift
Has not his flying-crooked gift.

— Robert Graves

CONTENTS

✈ ✈ ✈

PART 3—FOUR BARS

Appendixes

The Author's Journey

✈ ✈ ✈

Grant Corriveau has been an aviator, one way or another, for a long time. As a boy, he built plastic aircraft models and through the power of imagination, soared into the skies. Later in life, he learned to fly real, ***ragwing Fleet Canucks***, then moved on, step-by-step, towards ever larger and faster aircraft.

Along the way, as an instructor, he helped *uplift* others to see the joys and challenges of flight for themselves. One summer he seeded thunderstorms along the foothills of Alberta. Then he became an airline pilot, spending the next thirty years transporting people across North America and the Caribbean. Just before retiring, he built and flew his own kit airplane, and was thrilled to find that the wings stayed on throughout its first test flight.

Over the years, he has learned to be thankful for the many people who uplifted him along the way: family, friends, colleagues and strangers. He currently lives on Vancouver Island with his wife and greatest friend, France.

Though the body ages and he is reminded daily that "we are but dust," he also believes we are more than that. As Master Yoda observed: *"Luminous beings we are."* And Buzz Lightyear adds, *"To infinity and beyond!"*

The journey continues...

Prologue
A Value-Added Experience

✈   ✈   ✈

I have always been thrilled with airplanes and aviation. Looking back, my journey seems a little like the flight of a butterfly that can't travel six inches in a straight line—yet somehow, mysteriously migrates thousands of miles and arrives at one specific destination that was always there, waiting.

I believe we are all subject to and helped along by kindness during our journeys. I see how many others added value to my life in many ways, but maybe most clearly in my career as a pilot. I realize how this help and kindness from others *uplifted* me toward something greater than I could have become on my own.

I believe life is a "value-added" experience. We all start with something—things given us as at birth. At the very least, we were given life itself. I don't know why some of us seem to have won the deluxe versions, with all the bells and whistles, while others seem to have been blessed with lesser gifts. I do know, however, that what we choose to do with what we're given not only makes a major difference in how our lives turn out, but also affects everyone around us, either directly or indirectly, for better or worse.

All of us have gifts and opportunities or challenges in life—for no apparent reason—for nothing we deserve. Where do they come from? How do any of us account for these starting points?

I once built a recreational aircraft from a kit. I was searching for help in an online forum one day. Someone used the term "scratch builder," suggesting perhaps that his method—building the airplane from raw plans and not from a factory-supplied kit—made him a superior builder. I couldn't resist the bait—and promptly asked him what his method was for home-smelting aluminum. Where did he mine his bauxite ore? How did he fabricate his bolts, nuts, rivets and fasteners? How about his drills and other tools? Did he build these too?

I was obviously making the point that even if some builders—the so-called "scratch builders"—start working from a point closer to the beginning of a project, they are only one extremely small step earlier in a complex chain. We are merely adding value to the preceding accomplishments of others upon whom our society has risen. We should never take for granted the basic knowledge, the infrastructure and underlying organization that forms the foundation for all our subsequent endeavors.

Today, all aircraft designers build upon what went before. They can look up tables of specifications for the strength and capabilities of various materials. Then they can accurately determine the parameters for all components of an aircraft, ensuring each part will be strong enough for the stresses involved. They can calculate these stresses because of the development of theoretical and practical mathematics we all depend upon. Or, more likely today, we punch the data into a computer that does the complicated math for us. A computer that was also conceived, designed, built and programmed by many others. We all stand on the shoulders of those who came before. Then, if we are lucky, we too might contribute just a little to the growing pool of knowledge, experience and accomplishment.

When I read how Wilbur and Orville Wright built and became airborne in the first successful, controllable flying machine, I am in awe of their inspiration and determination. They too were building upon what came before. They could only build a successful aircraft because the science and technology of their day had advanced to the point where they could find the needed materials, tools, ideas and information about previous failed attempts. Then, after a lot of reading, talking, thinking, trying and failing, they solved the problems and designed a flying vehicle that could be continuously controlled in three dimensions. Next, even more remarkably, they climbed on board and taught themselves how to fly it—without killing themselves.

By contrast, I have always stepped into well-proven aircraft. I benefited from experiences of instructors, mechanics and others as I studied and practiced to become a pilot. I survived thousands of hours in the air—sometimes through very challenging conditions—because I was taught and mentored by so many great men and women who poured their efforts into my education and helped me become successful at my chosen field. Thankfully, later on in my career, I was able to pass on some little bits of what I'd learned to younger colleagues who followed me into the *flight decks.*

I hope to share my experiences with many who would have loved to have my job—but could not for various reasons. I've met a lot of people, pilots and non-pilots, who for one reason or another are working at jobs they don't really care for. Many of them became pilots, hoping to follow a similar career path to mine, but the timing didn't work out. When they were ready, the airlines were not hiring, so these folks had to move on. I hope they can glimpse some of the joys and challenges of airline flying.

Many could not take the gamble I took, investing tens of thousands of dollars and years of effort toward qualifying as a commercial pilot on the unlikely prospect that upon finishing a job might await. They could not commit to the years of striving to gain the required experience and then survive on meager pay and poor working conditions—and hope. Hope that eventually, they would catch the golden ring—the title *Captain* at a stable airline.

For every individual who successfully navigates their way through this labyrinth, hundreds of others must choose other paths. Yet they are curious about the life of an airline pilot. This is one reason flight simulation software is consistently on the best-seller list for home computers. Even though airline travel has become so normal and even mundane, the dream of sitting in the "pointy end" remains alive— flight controls in hand and the best view in the world surrounding you. For fans of aviation, I hope to share some of my adventures.

I don't know why I was the lucky one for whom the dream came together. I don't understand how life works and chance events come together for some of us, but not for others. It does fascinate me and gives me pause to wonder and question what life is all about. I guess that's why, to this day, my favorite aviation book is the classic *Fate is the Hunter* by Earnest K. Gann. You'll find a few other of my personal favorites listed near the end of this book.

My stories are usually drawn from looking back over my career, which has thankfully been fairly routine. Trust me: when you are flying on a commercial airliner, boring is good. You wouldn't like exciting. Consequently, my stories are not often about engines exploding, wheels falling off and airplanes catching fire. Though that kind of stuff goes on, thankfully it hasn't often been my experience. My stories are the more mundane things—the little things that inhabit real life.

My stories are true. Or at least I remember them happening. Given all we know today regarding the unreliability of human memory, while the underlying events and principles are probably accurate, some of the details may not be, and I've reconstructed the dialog for best literary effect.

My stories are not limited to any one airline. They are universal, so I do not mention which company I flew with. The characters in my stories are based on actual people. Sometimes I describe them in more detail—as far as I knew and understood them—but sometimes they are composite characters, representing a cross-section of the many intriguing individuals I've worked with.

The thoughts and opinions expressed are my own and do not necessarily reflect those of any other person, airline or entity.

I hope you enjoy reading my stories and meanderings as I retrace some of the steps in "this pilot's journey."

Grant Corriveau
2018

PART 1
The Sideways Pilot

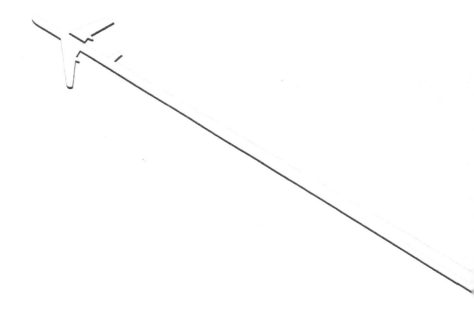

1

THREE GREEN—OOPS?

✈ ✈ ✈

When events take an unexpected turn, how do we cope?

Second Officer's Log:
1975, B727, YQR (Regina) Final Approach

I'm still a rookie *second officer* but even I know it's not supposed to happen like this.

The captain called *"Before Landing Check."* *That's normal.* The *FO (first officer)* and I moved the appropriate switches, levers and buttons, and chanted the usual incantations. *That's normal.* The trusty old Boeing 727 responded with its arcane dialect of flashing lights and flickering needles. *That's normal.* And the all-important landing gear panel is now showing three green lights assuring us that the wheels are locked down. *That's normal.* But the landing gear control panel is also glowering at us with a trio of red lights, telling us that the green lights are not to be trusted. *That's not normal!*

The captain swings into action. "Now look what you've done!" he accuses the first officer. "Recycle it!" The first officer, looking rather peevish, does so. He reaches to the center panel and returns the heavy gear handle to the up position as we watch expectantly. All the usual bumps, thunks and whirs express themselves from the bowels of the plane as several hundred pounds of landing gear assemblies and bulky doors tuck themselves away again. When all the lights extinguish and the commotion dies down, he then returns the handle to the down position and the extension noises erupt throughout the aircraft again, especially just below our feet where the nose-wheel is located.

As we await the outcome I think about how recycling is a *"Pilot's Favorite Remedy."* It provides a two-pronged approach to any aircraft abnormality. First, it will often cause the problem to just go away. Second, and more importantly, it stalls for time as we recover from the confusion of this unwelcome break in the routine and wonder what to

do if the problem persists. Which it does. We stare sullenly at the
bouquet of green and red lights glowing stubbornly from the landing
gear panel.

The captain now turns to me: "Checklist?"

I have been frantically flipping through the manual. Let an engine
quit, let a generator fail, let the gear not come down at all, that's okay.
We've got a printed routine or a scripted procedure to follow. But
nowhere in our extensive catalog of emergency and abnormal checklists
can I find anything to help explain why all the red lights and all the
green lights are on together, and which ones to believe.

"There's nothing here for that particular abnormality," I tell him,
"therefore, this can't be happening."

He flashes me a look that suggests he is re-evaluating his belief in
the relatively new concept of **Crew Resource Management**. He turns
back to the flight controls, pushes climb power back into the three
Pratt and Whitney turbojet engines and with gentle finesse born of
experience, eases the heavy Boeing skyward again. "Go Around," he
calls, triggering more actions from the first officer to reposition the
wing flaps and alert **ATC (air traffic control)**, "but leave the gear
down." He wants some time to sort this out before attempting to
reattach a hundred tons of airplane to the earth at a hundred and fifty
miles an hour. It's difficult to convince anyone that the touchdown
was merely firm when the wheels collapse after landing.

Now the situation drastically departs from the day-to-day routine
of **line flying**. It also departs from the routine scenarios of simulator
training, where I've gained most of my experience with abnormal procedures. I begin to realize just how many things the simulator doesn't
simulate—like other aircraft in the circuit or surprised air traffic controllers who wish you wouldn't do this as their pattern is full right
now. It doesn't simulate company dispatchers and local airport agents
who want a new **ETA (estimated time of arrival)**. It doesn't simulate
flight attendants who want to know what's happening, and if they
should inform the passengers or if you will tell them. Worst of all, neither line flying nor the simulator has prepared me for what I'm faced
with next as we circle the airport and the captain says to me, "You'd
better go back and check the viewing ports."

Now, wait a minute! I've only been on **the line** for two months, and when I looked through those little ports during training nobody said I'd ever have to do it for real. Well, maybe they hinted there might be a small chance someday, but I'm really not up to it today. Besides, the first officer is more experienced. Wouldn't you rather trust him to do it? And where are those little windows located anyhow? And worst of all, that cabin is full of passengers, and the simulator definitely never simulated passengers.

"On my way."

I wonder why I'm having difficulty standing up. Have my knees gone so weak at the thought of facing our customers in the midst of this potential crisis? I remember to unfasten my seat-belt. Ah, much better. I'm about to swing the cabin door open then realize my mind has gone blank regarding the exact location of the viewing ports. I picture myself running breathlessly back to the front end after ripping out all the carpets to ask, "Hey guys! Just where are those little window-things anyway?" It's not a pretty picture. I fumble with one last glance into the 'Quick Reference Handbook.'

Then I take a deep breath before heading into the cabin pausing to assume what I hope is an air of calm authority that will reassure nervous passengers. Swinging open the door I brace myself expecting to confront one hundred and thirty anxious faces. Fortunately, there are only four. Unfortunately, they're the flight attendants. This shakes my confidence, wondering what they know that I don't. The passengers are too preoccupied with the view of the city or their newspapers to notice me.

My calm air of authority begins to waver as I collapse to my knees, clawing at the carpet. I'm pretty sure one of the junior attendants makes a move towards the first aid oxygen, but the steady hand of a more experienced colleague stops her. It's just a new second officer falling apart under pressure—no big deal.

"What's happening? Can we help?" they inquire, stepping closer.

Get off the carpet! "Er ... it's just a small problem with an indicator. No sweat. Could you step back a little please?"

I peel back the industrial-strength tapestry to expose the round wooden cover and pry it loose. Then, pressing my nose against the floor while my rear end waves reassuringly towards the assembled crowd, I am barely able to see the two properly-aligned indicators through the dirty glass viewing port. The nose-wheel is locked down. Gathering what's left of my composure, I head further back into the cabin.

An elderly lady raises a hand to catch my attention and I prepare to calm her. "Excuse me, young man," she begins, "if this is going to take long, could I get another cup of coffee?" She's in much worse shape than she appears if she's prepared to drink another cup of airline coffee. I leave her in the capable hands of the flight attendant.

Then I'm on my knees excavating carpet again. The nearest seam is two rows away from the viewing ports and as I burrow along on my elbows, I suspect that my calm air of authority is lost forever. After confirming that the main wheels are also locked down, I retreat towards the sanctity of the cockpit exiting the cabin with a last graceful stumble—note for maintenance: get carpet fixed—and arrive back in my seat with a crash.

"All three gear are showing down and locked," I report.

The captain acknowledges this and as I slip my headset back on, I overhear the instructor of a military training jet which is sliding by along our left flank provide him with another confirmation. I wonder to myself briefly if the student is flying their jet while the instructor looks us over and just how good a student pilot he is and most of all— why is he flying so close to our airplane!

Meanwhile, the first officer is busy communicating with ATC as well as talking to our company maintenance personnel on the other radio. "Did you recycle it?" I hear them ask. Apparently, recycling is also a "Mechanic's Favorite Remedy." Grabbing my **QRH (quick reference handbook)**, I quickly work my way through the checklists ensuring that all is prepared once again for landing. I'm surprised at how quickly our low-level maneuvering is slurping up our contingency fuel. Landing with or without red lights is starting to seem like a very good idea.

As we roll out once again on the ***final approach track***, ATC confirms that the crash vehicles have been called out. An unfortunate choice of terms, I think to myself as I crane my neck for a view out the front window. I see a station wagon and a jeep with a fire extinguisher in the back. It's comforting to think that if the ***galley*** catches fire at least the crew meals might be saved—if we don't mind our steaks well done.

Now the captain scans the cockpit one last time. I figure he is checking with his mind's eye the intricate schematic diagrams of the landing gear system, calling upon his thousands of hours of experience and profound technical knowledge to provide the missing piece to this puzzle. I'm certain that any moment he will turn to us lesser mortals and reveal in a captainly manner why all the red lights can be on if the gear is, in fact, down and locked. Instead, he leans across the center console and gives the landing gear lever a sound inward thump. The micro-switch which senses the gear-handle position makes contact. Presto—all the red lights go out.

"Stupid thing," he remarks.

I am reminded of another *Pilots Favorite Remedy*—thumping. Of course, I think to myself. How many times have I used the same technique on a recalcitrant television or vending machine? Why should a multi-million-dollar airplane be any different?

"You should have thought of that earlier," he growls at us, "and saved all this nonsense. Oh, it's lonely at the top."

We land smoothly—well, not that smoothly—the captain assures us he just wanted to make certain the gear was truly locked down.

That's normal.

2

A Dime a Dozen

✈ ✈ ✈

My fingertips are aching. I'm sitting cross-legged on a mattress on the floor. It's April 1973 here at the university's married-students' residences where I live with my pregnant wife and 3-year-old son. Our makeshift couch and cement brick bookcases represent student-poverty-chic. My finger problem is related to the little mechanical typewriter perched on my lap where I am laboriously pecking away on a job application. I am hoping it will not look like it was typed by a six-year-old child, but that's unlikely when I'm constantly needing the white-out correction tape to hide my typos.

I pause for a moment to wonder why I'm about to make a fool of myself—why I am doing something I don't like doing—taking a risk. I'm not qualified for the job I'm applying for—yet. But for most of my life, I have been quietly holding onto a dream. I have decided that now I must either actualize that dream or put it to death. I will succeed wildly and rise to new heights or fail miserably and go down in flames—metaphorically speaking I hope—because what I'm about to do is apply to become a professional pilot and one day captain those big jets. I am going to take my best shot but I must face the truth: this is a long shot. A really long shot. In keeping with my conservative nature, I've given myself a deadline—an ETA if you will. Within two years I will either have landed a *Good Job* or I shall abandon the dream and find another way of making a living. The clock is ticking.

I've been enthralled by airplanes for as long as I can remember. Growing up next to a busy airport can do that to a young boy. From my bedroom window in the attic of our post-war story-and-a-half home, I would watch as lumbering C-119 *Flying Boxcars* and tiny flying club planes droned overhead to enter the landing pattern at the Edmonton airport. I also remember my prized plastic aircraft models. They were crudely built because I rushed through the assembly stage to start "flying" them. The wheels and propellers and canopies were over-glued into immobility and the decals torn and crooked, but through

9

the power of my imagination, they flew countless missions of daring and adventure.

When I was twelve-years-old, I was allowed to cycle with friends over to the airport and hang out on the observation deck. In those days, even a busy commercial airport was accessible to young aviation enthusiasts. We would drop our bikes at the bottom of the staircase and gallop to the rooftop deck. A green wooden bench gave us front row seats to the entire airport. We passed wonderful hours leaning over the steel railing, oohing and aahing at the exotic airliners. In 1962 these were the aging C46 *Commandos* and DC-3s that had done their duty in World War II. I recognized them from the documentaries my father watched on our grainy black and white TV. For those of us so lucky as to be born beyond the reach of war, these workhorse airplanes represented the hopes of a fledgling new airline industry. Our childish thrills could not be contained by mere TV images but instead swirled all around us in glorious three dimensions and living color. Our futures seemed as bright and loud and full of promise as the hectic world playing out right before us on the airport *tarmac*.

We would thrill to the screaming Vickers Viscount turbo-props that bathed us in warm fumes as they powered away from the terminal. Then the deep roar of an arriving Lockheed Super Constellation assailed us, its four huge radial engines spitting and popping as this elegant aircraft rumbled up and parked. If jet fumes were perfume, then engine noises were a pure symphony to my twelve-year-old senses. We watched with fascination as ramp crews swarmed the plane and passengers disembarked. We waited expectantly for the moment when the uniformed pilots would emerge from the aircraft's main door, stride confidently down the stairs and cross the ramp into the office below us. A few minutes later they'd reappear to begin their preparations for another departure.

I studied the pilots' movements as intently as I did all my sports heroes. I noticed how one of them always walked around the aircraft, inspecting it before heading back up the *air-stairs* to the cabin door. Soon the captain would appear at his sliding window and exchange mysterious hand signals to a crewman on the ramp. Then the co-pilot reached up to an unseen panel and one of the huge four-bladed propellers would slowly begin to rotate, laboriously at first but building up speed. A puff of black smoke and a pop and rumble and then more smoke and the propeller would accelerate into a flashing blur of silver in the sparkling sun. Finally, the engine would roar once and settle into a steady idle. The procedure was repeated three more times, adding to the glorious soundscape. A thumbs-up passed between pilot and ramp-man and then with a snarl like a wild animal reluctantly waking up, the engines surged and the plane pivoted on gangly landing gear and taxied away to the far end of the airport. The music of the engines faded slowly with distance.

We'd watch the majestic Lockheed pull silently onto the runway, followed soon by the faint roar of fully-powered engines as it accelerated and lofted itself free of earth. Any hint of awkwardness instantly vanished as the great airship returned to its natural environment and the wheels tucked away. I'd stare intently until it disappeared into the sky. Later that night—unable to sleep, sitting up in bed, still excited— I would re-enact the entire sequence, playing the part of the captain while producing a full array of engine sounds—but softly as to escape my mother's detection and her reminders to "Go to sleep!"

A few years later I was sitting at the family dinner table recounting my high school's career fair presentations. I described with guarded enthusiasm what I learned from a Boeing 707 captain of a local charter airline, Wardair. For the first time in my life, an airline captain became a real person and not just an icon. He bridged a gap between my imaginings and what might actually be possible. To my parents, I tentatively voiced the idea that I might like to become an airline pilot. "Pilots are a dime a dozen," my dad said. "Stay in school and get a *Good Job*." He wasn't wrong. Thousands of ex-air force pilots had flooded into civilian life in the two decades since World War II. Our nextdoor neighbor was a prime example. Unable to find a flying job, he was now selling Boeing-Vertol helicopters. I reluctantly pushed my flying dreams onto a back burner.

Roll the clock ahead to 1970. I'm twenty years old and I am in the coffee shop at the Edmonton Flying club, chatting with my instructor who just asked me "Why are you learning to fly?" I thought about my life-long interest and how, thanks to a gift from my wife and her father, I was now working my way towards a recreational private pilot's license. I tentatively explained how I sometimes wondered if perhaps maybe there was an outside chance that someday possibly I might like to try to fly commercially—sort of. The dousing of cold water came quickly. "Pilots are a dime a dozen," he said. And he wasn't wrong. American Airlines was in the news that week, announcing massive layoffs of pilots. Other carriers were on the verge of doing the same. "Stay in university," he said. "Get a *Good Job*—become a lawyer or a doctor," he said. "Just fly for fun." So again, I reluctantly pushed my dream aside.

Over the next couple of years, I tried the "stay-in-school and get a *Good Job*" strategy, but it wasn't working out. I hated being cooped up in classrooms all day. Wasn't twelve years enough already? I was pretty sure I needed to work outdoors at something that engaged my body as well as my mind.

I took a year off school and tried my hand at more physical labor. I worked on the railroad, installing signaling equipment along the tracks between Edmonton and Jasper. Swinging a pickaxe into a frozen gravel roadbed while the foreman shouted, "Dig ya bastards! Ya wouldn't go to school—now dig!" inspired me to rethink my options. I went back to university but kept discovering I was unsuited for so many things. I still wanted to fly. I gradually concluded that I had to at least try. Unless I tried, I'd never know what could happen.

Piloting captivated me both intellectually and physically in the dynamic, ever-changing experience that is flying. Only flying lit the fire within. But my father and my flying instructor had not been wrong in their warnings that pilots are a dime a dozen. The landscape was littered with folks who dreamed of careers as pilots. Somehow they came up with the substantial financial resources to chase their dream. As a young married man with 1.5 children, I was uncertain how I could proceed. I only knew it was time to take my best shot or abandon the dream forever.

3

DO, OR DO NOT

✈   ✈   ✈

Aviation is a funny business. For every *Good Job,* there are hundreds of others where the pay is ridiculously low, especially considering the cost of obtaining the credentials. The working conditions in these underpaid jobs are dangerous. Pilots are often pressured to fly under-maintained aircraft in marginal weather because "if you won't do it, someone else will." And yet because flying is a passion for most pilots, employers enjoy a steady stream of applicants.

I don't recall the exact moment when I decided to take my shot at a career as a pilot. But according to my logbook, two life-altering events occurred in the spring of '73. First, I earned my commercial license. It's the ticket that allows a pilot to fly for hire. But at this point, without advanced qualifications and experience, no one will hire you. Second, my daughter was born, rounding up the number of children to an even two. I noticed how this was much easier to express on job application forms.

Initially, my job applications said something like "I don't yet meet your minimum requirements, but now I have a commercial license and I'll keep you updated as I acquire the remaining credentials." On one hand, I felt very silly applying for jobs that I wasn't qualified for, but on the other hand, I'd watched and hopefully learned something from my friend Rick. He was what I'd call a "go-getter." Rick set his mind on a goal, then with an unflagging sense of optimism, he started working his way toward it. I wanted to emulate him, but I didn't have his social skills. Yet my longing to fly continually challenged my introverted nature and I began a friendly siege of the aviation industry.

In Canada in the 1970s, the *Good Jobs* were available at only a handful of airlines operating jet transport aircraft. There were also a few corporate flight divisions operating business jets and turbo-prop planes. I knew that some pilots also made a career flying in the military. I loved the thought of flying those high-performance fighters and transports, but I was pretty sure that my fear of bullets might hold me back. After one short interview at my local recruiting office, I put the military option aside for the time being.

So apart from military flying, there were two pathways to the *Good Jobs*. The first was through a handful of colleges around the country giving pilot training, coordinated with a two or three-year college diploma. However, none of these schools were near me. As a husband and father, I was not prepared to hike off across the country.

The second way—the route I chose—was to pay my way at the local flight school. This was a very expensive option. There were no student loans available so I faced the prospect of selling all my assets. I got about ten dollars for my old bike. Thankfully other resources such as the "Bank of Family" were much more helpful. I couldn't have done it without this generous aid.

I also knew that a university degree would make my application more competitive and count for extra points on the airlines' evaluation schemes. You don't need a university degree to fly planes, but it proves that you can at least learn theoretical subjects quickly and it helps the airlines sort through their piles of applicants. I had already completed one year of university. I transferred into the geography department and immediately signed up for cartography and meteorology courses. Those were a slam-dunk. Programs in statistics and even northern geography also gave me useful information and skills. There was a generous student loan program available for university and I took full advantage.

Beyond this, I needed to create my own aviation-oriented curriculum. I started devouring every book connected to aviation that I could find in every library in the city.

As for my flight credentials, I continued chipping away on these as funds allowed. Within a few months, I obtained a ***Flight Instructor's Rating***. Suddenly I could get paid for flying! Finally, I was on the way. I had a foot in the door—my first step hopefully towards "the big jets." On the horizon, I still needed the ***instrument rating*** and the endorsement to fly multi-engined aircraft. Then the biggest obstacle loomed—landing that first job. No one would hire a pilot without experience, but I couldn't get experience until someone hired me. Can you say "Catch 22"?

Roll the scene back to that day in 1973 when I sat on our makeshift sofa, plunking away on the second-hand typewriter. I had a commercial pilot's license and a dream. And now I felt like I could start forcing my toes into the doorways for the few *Good Jobs*. "This month I added ten more hours of flying experience. I passed my written tests for my **instrument flying** rating. I read the following books on aviation... Please update my resume, thanks. Yours truly . . ."

When I look back on the process, I remember the hopes and doubts. My hopes were encapsulated by Yoda from the Star Wars movies. At one point, Jedi master Yoda counsels a doubting Luke Skywalker to "Do, or do not. There is no try." But against this kind of emotional certitude, my doubts assailed me. I was being presumptuous. I feared the airline staff who dealt with my trivial update letters each month would see me as a nuisance. As TV character Homer Simpson once said, "I hate trying. Trying is just the first step towards failure." Thankfully, I was driven so strongly by my desire to become an airline captain—to fly the big jets—that I pushed past my Homer and clung to my Yoda.

Flash ahead a year and a half. I'm sitting in an office at the Vancouver International Airport about to start an interview for my dream job. My imaginary deadline clock is ticking loudly, nearing midnight. Behind an imposing executive desk, the **Base Flight Operations Director** and his **chief pilot** are pouring over papers and shuffling documents. I am one of many candidates being interviewed this day. The Director pulls a fat manila folder from his drawer. My name is scrawled on it in black felt pen. He drops it onto his desk with a heavy thud. He glances at me, smiling wryly, and says, "Someone's been busy."

The interview goes well.

4

One in Three

✈ ✈ ✈

Bam! A pile of company manuals, forms and other reading material lands on my desk. I'm sitting in a classroom with about two dozen other *new-hire pilots* at the airline's training center.

"Look around the room at your fellow candidates. Only one in three of you will make it to the normal retirement age. The other two will drop out along the way. Some will develop medical complications that will invalidate their pilot's licenses. They'll be grounded. Others will fail a training course as they progress towards a captain's job. They'll be fired. Everyone is expected to eventually become captains. We do not employ permanent first-officers.

"Others will be let go because they are unable to maintain required standards during recurrent training, either in the simulator or on the line. Others will simply find the job too stressful—can't deal with the pressure of being continually tested and checked. Some will grow weary of working irregular schedules that undermine any semblance of normal family life. They will retire early."

The speaker pauses to consult his notes and let this information sink in. Mr. McPlane is our Human Resources representative. We listen attentively from our assigned desks in the institutional gray and beige classroom. We're in the upper story of the airline's Montreal facility. He continues to introduce us to the realities of our chosen profession. He describes our place in the company hierarchy—low, really low.

"Get used to it," he cautions. "You have a long way to go before you attain the exalted status and are addressed as 'Captain.'" He details what is expected of us as the employees of a proud corporation with a long history and hard-won international reputation for excellence. He dwells especially on the ways we might fail to survive our six-month probationary period, let alone a full career.

"If you are lucky and things go well, you will finally become a captain in the last few years of your career. At last, you will earn the

17

big bucks you're dreaming of. Only those of you who are currently under twenty years of age will be around long enough to make it to the first page of the seniority list. If you do, you might have a chance at the top-paying job as a captain on our largest aircraft, the 747." Only two in our classroom are so young. I am nearer the average age of twenty-five.

Next, we address the paperwork. We begin with ominous forms to designate our next of kin. I read references to 'death or dismemberment.' Wait a minute! Did I miss something? I thought airline flying was safe. My perceptions will be shaken again in a few months when I try to buy life insurance and discover that I have to pay a higher premium than non-pilots. I wonder what the insurance industry knows. What aren't they telling the rest of us? We go on to fill out forms for pension plan enrollment, unemployment insurance and union membership. We write down social insurance numbers, phone numbers and addresses again and again.

All the while, McPlane continues describing details of our lives as airline employees. He talks about guest lecturers we are to expect. I begin to feel like Charles Dickens' Scrooge when he is forewarned of his soon-arriving phantasmal Christmas Eve visitors. Our specters will explain the intricacies of crew scheduling, flight dispatching, union rules, duty limitations, time-rigs and payscales. While none of our visitations will be as dire as Scrooge's, they are nevertheless intended to convert us—not from death to life but from outsiders to insiders— into pilots who will one day be trusted with the keys to a multi-million-dollar airliner full of precious customers and all the associated risks and liabilities. We will either be transformed into model airline-captains-to-be or, like Scrooge, face our doom. While Scrooge must face his own mortality in the guise of a tombstone with his own name inscribed, we face the vision of our training files stamped with "Ceased Training" in large red letters marking the mortality of our dreams. Our epitaphs will simply say: NOT GOOD ENOUGH.

Over the subsequent weeks, the information onslaught is unrelenting and the term "drinking from a firehose" will be used often. That only begins to describe this experience of the new-hire pilots indoctrination course. Over the next six weeks, we will strive to absorb the intricacies of high altitude jet airliner operations, learn about jet streams and upper fronts and high altitude meteorology. We will be introduced to aircraft pressurization systems, complex hydraulic systems, ice and rain protection systems and electrical systems. The specifics of any particular airliner will be saved for later and then learned in excruciating detail. But for now, it is enough that we expand our minds beyond the relatively simple one or two-engine light aircraft that most of us have been flying.

On this first day, standing erect and proud at the front of the classroom is Trevor, a retired captain from Air India. He is our lead instructor. He exudes a vague air of royalty. I easily imagine him as one of those old-school captains who have been known to don white gloves as they take their seat at the controls of the new generation of jetliners that are transforming the air transportation world. Near him is Garth, leaning against the front wall, looking much like the "good cop" to Trevor's "bad cop." He flew with the Pakistani Air Force and later, with their national airline. He grins easily and when he talks, his language is plain, earthy and to the point. He will tell you exactly what he thinks and his assessment will invariably be firm but fair. He is a man without artifice and that alone makes him an excellent teacher. These two men are tasked with shepherding the *new-hires* and they do so with infinite patience, wisdom and thankfully, a good dose of humor. Whatever failures we experience will be our own and not due to a lack of quality instruction.

Together, they will try to install in our sodden brains the mysteries of high-bypass jet engines, compressors and turbines, how they work and how they fail. They will insist we understand frightening new terms like *"compressor stalls," "hung starts"* and *"hot starts."* They tell us about the dangers of high altitudes and the challenges to jet airplane operations. We will wrestle with concepts like *"high-speed buffet"* and something horrifically called *"coffin corner"!*

We will learn transatlantic navigation principles, study ditching techniques and inflate life jackets and escape slides. We will practice the operation of rescue beacons and survival packs against that day we hope never comes—when we might end up floating and freezing on the open oceans, awaiting rescue. More sobering still, we will learn about firefighting on board airliners.

More than once I will envy my coursemates who have either

military or corporate jet experience. They are already familiar with this material. We, the great unwashed civilian charter pilots, flight instructors and recent flying school graduates, have only encountered these concepts theoretically while studying for our commercial licenses. Our more advanced co-learners have already flown into the upper regions above 18,000 feet where altitudes are called *flight levels*. They are already familiar with these upper reaches of the sky where airliners and eventually we too will routinely go—one day.

For now, Mr. McPlane continues to step us through the airline indoctrination portion of today's program. Day One is eventually finished. One down, many more to go. Did I mention "drinking from a firehose?" I'm already on the verge of drowning, but feeling deliriously happy and fortunate to be here. This giddiness overarches everything—even the recurring moments of self-doubt when I fear they will discover I was hired by mistake, that I am a sham and not at all worthy. One in three, McPlane said. I can't help smiling. This represents a big improvement over "a dime a dozen" I'd once been told was a pilot's worth. Things are looking up.

5

Heck of a Ride

✈   ✈   ✈

"There's a truck on the runway!
Abort the takeoff! Abort the takeoff!"

We didn't need to hear it twice. Captain Gregg slammed the B727 **thrust levers** closed, yanked the ground spoiler lever back and stomped on the brakes as hard as he could. FO (First Officer) Erwing yanked the reverse thrust levers to the **vertical detents**. Amber lights illuminated on the front panel and pierced the darkened flight deck—Erwing announced "Reverse deployed." Captain Gregg fumbled in the dark for the levers and hauled back fully on all three. Or at least he meant to.

Maybe it was because he was accustomed to only two reverse thrust levers on the DC-9. Maybe it was because he hadn't yet adequately adjusted his grip, to the longer levers on this Boeing. Or maybe it was because in the darkness of a flight deck configured for our midnight departure from **LAX** (Los Angeles International Airport), his hand just slipped. For whatever reason, number three reverser stayed at idle while one and two suddenly flared to full negative thrust. I watched helplessly from my second officer's chair as first officer Erwing fumbled along with Captain Gregg to re-establish symmetrical power.

Meanwhile, the ponderous 727 swerved towards the left-side runway lights that were blurring past our windows. We heard a sickening screech from our nosewheel as the captain tried to compensate with the steering pedals. I was flung against my seatbelt as my shoes scrambled to find grip on the shiny metal floor and I braced my hands against anything they could find. Books and pens and flight bags and everything else not tied down began sliding and tumbling along the floor as we decelerated under the impressive force of brakes and roaring JT8D engines. Then we felt rumbling and shaking as our left main wheels wandered off the concrete.

Our landing light beams swept over the dark gray pavement, revealing scattered tire marks and painted runway lines. These seemed to swirl past the first officer's window as the aircraft over-corrected and *yawed* wildly to the right as we kept skidding off the left edge of the pavement further into the infield. An old driving school admonition played in my head: "Steer into the skid." Too late. The airplane finally shuddered to a halt off the left side of the runway, facing ninety degrees across it.

We all sat there in stunned silence. All of us that is except the instructor. "Well, that was a *heck of a ride*," he chuckled as he reached forward and began resetting the controls and tapping commands into his keypad. "Thank goodness for flight simulators." The visual system flashed blank for a moment, then swooped us back into our original takeoff starting point at the button of the runway.

"Set the parking brake. We'll reconfigure and try that again." My first-ever flight simulator training course was off to an *interesting* start—if by *interesting* we are referring to that ancient curse, *"May you live in interesting times."*

The instructor was right on. It had been a *heck of a ride*. I was shocked by the deceleration rate of this 200,000-lb. aircraft, albeit simulated. But the point of simulation is, after all, to give an accurate representation of the event. I retrieved my pen, fuel log and sundry items that had skidded off the work table and lodged themselves behind the rudder pedals. I reorganized everything more securely against future assaults by the simulator's motion system. It all happened so fast. So much for our first rejected takeoff rehearsal. Over the next two weeks, we had many more opportunities to work out the kinks.

6

Full Flight Simulator in LAX

✈ ✈ ✈

Complex transport aircraft are flown by crews who must function cohesively, each knowing their duties as well as what to expect of their teammates. *SOPs (Standard Operating Procedures)* are at the heart of how we do this. Each crew member's tasks are carefully scripted and must be memorized and understood. When our training is complete, we will not only function smoothly as a team, but each of us will also become interchangeable. We can integrate with other crews we've never met when we transition to the regular line service.

So, the next step in our transition began. Our new-hire course ended and our aircraft conversion course began. From individual pilots with various backgrounds, differences and abilities, we were now to become members of a well-oiled team. The graduates of our class were assigned to become second officers on Boeing 727s. As such, we were teamed up with specific captains and first officers. Together, each trio began learning their individual roles and combining them to operate the Boeing 727.

Phase one was *Ground School,* an aviation colloquialism referring to the things we must learn before moving on to flight simulators. But as a new-hire pilot, I had much more to learn along with all this. Every airline has its own culture—its own jargon, unwritten standards and ways of doing things. I looked to my new captain and first officer colleagues for constant help in adjusting to my new "clan."

The B727s, like all first-generation jet transports, required three crew members. Along with the captain and first officer (pilot and co-pilot), who occupy the left and right seats respectively, a third crew member sits behind them and operates the systems control panel. Some airlines use an aviation mechanic in this role—their title is *flight engineer*. Other airlines have no need of such an aviation mechanic, so they assign pilots the job. This non-flying position is usually an entry-level job, staffed by junior pilots who hope to be promoted to a first officer's job and return to flying as soon as possible. In the meantime, they are known by many names. Some of them, in the tradition of welcoming the "new kids on the block" with good-natured hazing, are quite rude. But their official title is *second officer*.

In the 1970s, three-crew-member aircraft were being phased out. Like the navigators before them, the flight engineers and second officers were becoming redundant as more automated airplanes requiring only two pilots were becoming the new standard. Whether by twos or threes, in ground school we learned to function as a coordinated team.

The 1970s were also a time when ***Computer-Based Training*** concepts made inroads into airline training. Instead of group lectures, pilots worked through interactive, computer-driven lessons in our own cubicles, at our own pace. Here, we learned the technical details of our aircraft and how to operate them in both normal and abnormal situations.

At scheduled intervals, we'd collectively gather with the instructor, rehearsing all our ramp-to-ramp procedures as a crew in the so-called ***Paper Tigers***. We would sit in our respective positions before this panel mock-up to practice the operational flows and checks. All the while, we would talk our way through each procedure, pointing out all applicable switches or instruments and pausing often to question or discuss details with the instructor. Gradually we memorized the ***SOPs***, actions and required verbal calls for each stage of a flight. Soon we could describe every step of our duties by memory, from the moment we would board an aircraft and prepare it for flight, down to the last item of the shutdown checklist at our destination. Along with our *Paper Tiger* time, we also spent class time with the instructor digging into the intricacies of performance charts, graphs and planning procedures for the 727.

By the end of ground school, we had a good theoretical understanding of our Boeing 727. Now it was time to put this into practice.

The ***FFS (Full Flight Simulator)*** phase of training came next. Here we moved one step closer to reality and actual flights.

Our company did not have enough 727 simulators to keep up with the current training binge, so they had to rent time elsewhere. Continental Airways was a big operator of Boeing tri-jets and consequently, had slots to sell at their training center in Los Angeles. We were still in the depths of a Canadian winter, so this relocation to the west coast for our next phase was the good news. The bad news was the schedule. Like all airlines, Continental kept the preferred daytime sessions for their own crews and sold off the less desirable, wee-small-hours to others. Most of our training was to be conducted between 4 pm and 8 am. Did I mention that I'm actually not a nocturnal creature? Or that failure at any stage of the training would be cause for termination of my employment?

These oddball hours proved to be the first of many training challenges throughout my career. Simulator sessions themselves were exhausting. They were comprised of four intense hours of work with perhaps one short "pee break" in the middle. We were constantly busy, working through one irregularity or emergency after another, always expected to absorb another firehose flood of information, routines and procedures. These sessions were sandwiched between two long *briefings*. The pre-flight session usually took 90 minutes. The post-flight briefing would vary, but an hour was common. By the end of each lesson, I could barely remember all that we'd covered. I'd sit in the debriefing room, exhausted, staring at a clock that seemed twelve hours out of whack. I wondered what these intensive, item-by-item reviews of our shortcomings over the past hours were accomplishing. All I wanted by then was bed and sleep—and it didn't have to be in that order.

All our crews were housed at the local Ramada, so we passed one another on the way in and out of the hotel lobby or the training center. It was often hard to tell which crew looked worse—the one just going into the *sim (simulator)*, yawning heavily, struggling with sleep disruption and deprivation, or the one coming out and looking haggard, beat up and longing to hit the sack. During our brief conversations in passing, I listened for hints as to how these other crews were faring, wondering if we were keeping up. I could tell that our team was not the only one struggling with the offbeat hours.

One afternoon when First Officer Ewing and I really needed a break, we rented a car and took a tour through Beverly Hills and Marina Del Rey. We got to enjoy our *good news* assignment to sunny California for at least a few hours. Otherwise, all my spare time between *sim sessions* with Captain Gregg and First Officer Erwing was spent reading the manuals, memorizing the required drills and studying to stay on top of the material.

The days and nights following that first disastrous rejected takeoff and embarrassed slide into the airport infield went more smoothly. We eventually developed into a well-coordinated crew, able to handle all that was thrown at us. And they threw a lot at us. Over those two weeks, we faced engine failures, fires and an array of electrical problems and hydraulic system issues. We worked together to overcome landing gear problems, pressurization problems and emergency descents. We covered every technical failure that could conceivably occur on a Boeing 727 until we had mastered each one. We always worked under time constraints. If we messed up, the instructor would compress some other part of the lesson so we could have a second try. If we didn't get it right the second time, we knew things would become tense. The course was carefully planned, with very little wiggle room for extra practice. Extensions would require a complex re-shuffling of other crews' schedules.

After several days, tension among our crews grew as we learned that the course was going badly for one senior, respected captain. He could not adjust to the offbeat hours, fell behind and was sent home. Later, he was given another course with more "humane" learning hours and did fine. However, second chances were never guaranteed, especially for new-hire second officers. Sleep or no sleep, nothing but my maximum effort was good enough.

By the last days, the stress of that news and our growing fatigue was showing. One early morning, several members of various crews and their instructors were chatting in the hotel lobby. Some were heading for breakfast, others on their way to the training center. A second officer from another crew arrived from an overnight session, stumbled from the shuttle bus into the lobby and, shaking his head, said, "Gee, if I'd known so many things would go wrong, I'd have taken a later flight." We all broke into a fit of laughter, revealing how tense and sleep deprived most of us felt.

When the day of our ultimate simulator flight test arrived, our crew barely felt ready, but our instructor assured us we would do fine. Happily, the best, *almost* daytime slots were reserved for the flight tests. A Transport Canada inspector joined us and put us through the paces to prove what we'd learned. In the end, our crew passed, along with the others whose schedules intertwined with our own.

Our crew dispersed back to our homes for a few needed days off, followed by three days of *flying circuits* at the Halifax airport. When that was finally finished, I was ready to be assigned to the line to begin my new career.

7

Bolted to the Floor, Facing North

✈ ✈ ✈

Crude flight training devices, such as the venerable *Link Trainer,* were around since World War II. These little "sweat boxes," equipped with only basic instruments, were used for introducing pilots to the mysteries of instrument flying. Modern, so-called full-flight simulators (FFS) came of age in the 1970s. That's when computers became affordable and powerful enough to accurately model the aerodynamics of particular aircraft types. The nuances of takeoffs and landings, however, demanded more than this generation of devices could deliver. Before they could transport passengers, pilots still needed to perfect their skills in actual aircraft.

The sight of multi-million dollar jetliners flying circuits around the local airport, costing money instead of earning it, drove airline accountants into a frenzy. But concern for accountants' mental health was only a secondary reason the airlines were prepared to fund this new technology. They knew better simulators would quickly pay for themselves in other ways, as well. They reduced the number of accidents during flight training. Practicing emergencies at low altitude is risky business.

Besides economics and safety, simulators produced a better quality of training. With simulators, pilots could practice maneuvers in greater detail than we could in the airplane. Along with engine failures at the most critical times—during takeoffs and landings—now we practiced flying in the worst visibility, with fog and rain and wind made to order. Flight crews became better prepared than ever to handle the situations reality might throw at us. This eventually translated into better airline safety records.

Top-rated simulators are very good at convincing pilots they are flying the real thing. The instrument panels and hardware comprising the flight deck are extremely accurate, often built with the same components as the assembly-line aircraft. Hydraulically-powered motion systems reproduce key sensations. We feel turbulence and see its effect on our instruments. We feel accelerations when we increase the thrust and deceleration when applying brakes. Detailed sounds and vibrations are accurately modeled as well. The most convincing elements are created with the visual system. When we look out the windows, we see a synthesized world that closely resembles reality. Details like skid marks on the pavement, variations of fog, runway lights and the street lamps of the surrounding city all add to the illusion and convince our minds that *this is real*.

By the 1990s, the best flight simulators were becoming so accurate that pilots no longer required actual hands-on time when converting to a new aircraft type from something similar. When we finally strapped on the real thing, it was on a scheduled flight with a cabinload of un-suspecting passengers tagging along. However, we were still being watched carefully by an experienced training captain sitting beside us. Have you ever seen grocery store cashiers wearing badges proclaiming: *Please be patient—I'm learning*? Many times, I thought about making up a similar badge for my early flights on a new aircraft. But I resis-ted—frightening away nervous passengers is frowned upon by airline managers.

Despite the best features flight simulators could offer, some pilots had trouble adjusting. I recall one senior captain complaining, "They want me to believe this contraption is at 30,000 feet going west, but I know for a fact—*it's bolted to the floor facing north*."

8

Transitions and Transactions

✈ ✈ ✈

Womb to tomb—life is a transition.
The moment we are conceived, we begin changing.

A pilot's time as first or second officer is an apprenticeship. We strive toward the day when the seniority numbers give us our chance to be deemed worthy of a fourth stripe, the symbol of captaincy. Besides seniority, two elements control our career advancement: experience and training.

Experience is measured in hours aloft. Our logbooks are the repository for each precious minute of flight. Each entry is like a gold coin hoarded in a treasure chest. We are subsequently measured and evaluated by the weight of the chest. Each hour is a commodity. An hour of flight in a complex, fast or heavy aircraft is more valuable and weighty than the same hour spent flying basic trainers.

Training is measured with permits, licenses, ratings and endorsements. Along with the weight of our logbooks, our worth is calculated by the documents we carry, like so much paper currency. We are continually trying to add to our stash. A student-pilot permit becomes a private pilot's license. To this we may add a night endorsement, authorizing us to explore the challenges of dark flight. This is eventually upgraded through the painstaking and expensive effort to obtain a commercial license, to which we add a multi-engine rating and an instrument rating. These authorize us to charge for our services, manage extra engines and fly beyond sight of land. Along the way, hopefully, we will add aircraft-type endorsements as often as possible, expanding our ability to fly more demanding aircraft. Ultimately, when experience and training converge at the specified requirements, we attain the coveted *Airline Transport Pilot License (ATPL)*. Most of these licenses, qualifications and experiences must be gained—and paid for—on our own before the airlines will consider hiring us. Then we are ready to launch into the next stage of our ongoing journey. Our climb.

Our uplift.

The new-hire course was only the first of many transitions I would be required to survive in my new life as a professional airline pilot. Passing the new-hire course confirmed my status as an employee, officially authorizing me to occupy company premises. More importantly, to my creditors at least, it also placed me on the company payroll. In exchange, I had to do my part: always keep my hair neat, uniform clean, shirts pressed and shoes shined. Show up on time, be polite to passengers and never crash company airplanes. *Especially, never crash our airplanes.*

Each stage of advancement was demanding but paid dividends in the form of greater authority. And often bigger paychecks—let's not forget the paychecks.

My B727 conversion course was the next step on the ladder. I was now qualified to act as second officer on one specific type of plane. In return, I was expected to function as a full-fledged member of an operating crew: always respect the captain's authority, keep the fuel flowing and the engines running. Keep hydraulic pumps pumping and generators generating. Keep the cabins at a nice temperature and always manage the pressurization just right to keep everyone conscious. *Especially, keep everyone conscious.*

There was little apparent evidence of my newly-exalted status, aside from the crisp new uniform with its coded insignia, understood mainly by other pilots. Yet, it was the uniform that drove home a message to me. My decorated image, glimpsed in reflections in airport windows, reminded me that something important had changed. Upon entering the aircraft, rather than turning right into the passenger cabin, I now turned towards the front. There on the flight deck door, a sign in bold red letters announced: *Authorized Personnel Only.* By the simple act of opening that door, I claimed to be authorized—accredited by power from on high. Over the course of my career, no one ever challenged me for opening that door. Such was the power of the uniform.

9

Coldest Flight of the Year

✈   ✈   ✈

Second Officer's Log:
Winter 1976 / B727 / YWG (Winnipeg) Departure Gate

Arctic air gripped the prairies as Winnipeg's overnight temperature plummeted to -40°. A frigid wind sucked heat from everything it touched, including our Boeing 727. I peered at it through my reflection in the boarding lounge window. The plane sat frozen in pools of feeble yellow light that seeped from terminal building fixtures into the morning darkness. Snow swirls drifted and snaked across the frozen concrete, depositing hard mounds of snow around the aircraft's tires. The aerodynamic curves of our plane looked more like an ice sculpture than a flying machine. But a flying machine it was and this morning it was scheduled for an urgent mission: to "rescue" our crew and a load of hopeful passengers from the depths of a Winnipeg winter and deliver us to the gentler climes of San Francisco.

As I made my way down the bridge, hunching my shoulders against the bone-chilling cold, I was puzzled. Why was the plane still dead, dark and frozen this close to departure time? I had expected the ramp crews to have the lights on and the heat turned up full blast. Suddenly, at the far end of the walkway, the ramp door swung open and a burst of snow swooshed in with a wintery blast, propelling a parka-clad agent. He spotted me, waved a greeting and headed towards me. He was holding the bare heel of his other hand against his frozen cheek.

"The ramp equipment wouldn't start. None of it. Not the *GPU [Ground Power Unit]*, not the heater, and so far, not even the pushback tractor."

"Maybe the *APU [auxiliary power unit]* will start," I said, doubtfully. The B727 APU was infamously unreliable at starting in cold weather. I thought of the cozy bed I'd left at home and wondered if I'd be seeing the warm waves of the Pacific Ocean today after all.

I led the way into the dim flight deck where I fumbled for a flashlight. Starting an airliner is a cascading process. Everything depends on one little battery that cranks the APU turbine. Once this starts, the APU electrical generator brings to life all the lights, controls and switches. The APU compressor supplies *"bleed air"* to heat the cabin and more importantly, to spin our main engines at startup time.

However, before starting the APU there is a critical test required. The integrity of the fire protection system must be verified. This test is required because no one likes carrying flammable liquids on board an aircraft, but it has been determined—and often confirmed by inattentive pilots—that engines won't run without a steady supply of highly-flammable jet fuel. Designers mitigate this risk by installing automatic detection systems that watch for uncontained fires and put them out. As it happens, starting turbines in extremely cold weather is known for increasing the chances of starting just such fires. So, I dutifully pressed the test-switch.

Nothing. I held the test-switch longer. Still nothing. The icy-cold sensors, driven by a half-hearted, totally frozen APU battery, could not generate enough heat to trigger the test. I thought about starting the APU anyway. But as a new second officer, with a brand new mortgage on a modest house in the suburbs, I reckoned that burning an aircraft to the ground was a "bad thing" and should be avoided. Employers are fussy about stuff like that. Paying back the cost of a torched plane from my paltry new pilot paychecks would take a long time—a very long time.

Instead, we called for the mechanic. Within minutes a burly, bundled-up form tromped into the flight deck, pulling off ice-encrusted leather mitts and his breath-frosted snorkel-hood. "I just got the pushback tractor going. Now, what did you guys break?" He looked irked, anticipating yet another cold-related problem about to be dropped in his lap. I explained. He reached over and hit the APU start button, ignoring the fire-protection test. He apparently had no mortgage to pay nor job security issues—and little fear of fire. But the frozen battery could barely crank the turbine. It would not spin fast enough to properly initiate the start sequence.

We were stumped and stuck in Winnipeg. We retreated into the bridge just as Captain Dal and FO Bear arrived with our flight attendant crew close behind. We all huddled together taking stock. We had no electrical power from the ground power unit. No APU. No heat source to raise the cabin temperature to a survivable level. The Shell fuel-truck driver showed up and chimed in. Without electrical power, he couldn't load our fuel. Our coveted February layover in San Francisco was definitely in jeopardy. Minus 40 is a powerful motivator to get out of Winnipeg, so we scratched our heads looking for solutions. Everyone seemed highly motivated to find a solution, so I shivered in silence and refrained from suggesting that we just forget everything and head home to hibernate until spring.

Then an idea burbled to the surface of my sleepy brain. "If we had an air starter," I said, then hesitated as I realized everyone had turned to look at me. Apparently, I was using my "out loud voice" and was now committed to sharing the thought, no matter how silly it suddenly felt. "Could we get one main engine going and use it like a big APU...?" I trailed off. Even as I said it, it seemed like a strange idea. I was vaguely remembering an alternative method for starting jet engines. What we needed was a high-pressure air cart. Many airports still had these kicking around. The older jetliners from the 1960s, like the DC8s and 707s, depended on them because they lacked APUs. However, running a main engine for an extended period while parked at the gate was an unusual idea and nothing we'd learned in ground school. There was definitely no SOP for the situation we faced this morning.

The mechanic turned to the *ramp agent*, "Don't we have an old air cart stored somewhere behind the big hangar?" Then he said to Captain Dal, "How badly do you want to dangle your toes in the ocean today?" Captain Dal nodded enthusiastically. "Well, then let's try it," the mechanic said. He turned to leave with the ramp agent. "Let's see if we can dig it out." The winter-warriors trundled off into the bitter cold. The rest of us watched them go as we shifted from foot to frozen foot in our summer shoes, wondering what to do next. This was un-charted water. From here we would be creatively addressing issues one step at a time.

Our flight attendants shuffled back to the warmth of the lounge to plan their strategy. We three pilots dragged ourselves and our baggage into the flight deck, shivering in our skimpy airline overcoats. We kept these on, along with our hats, stowing our flight cases beside our chairs and climbing in, as if we were actually going flying—which was still highly doubtful. As I glanced at my colleagues in the front seats, it's the only time, other than in a low-budget Hollywood movie, that I ever saw pilots sitting at the controls wearing full uniforms. Anything to ward off the cold. FO Bear pulled a toque (the Canadian term for beanie) from his flight bag and donned that too. I couldn't help smiling. We looked more like a comedy team filming a TV sketch than a professional flight crew.

After a short discussion, Captain Dal laid out our plan and we began preparations. As I settled into my workstation, fractured songs played from the jukebox inside my head. Tony Bennett left his heart, then cross-faded to Eric Burden finding no place left to go, followed by Scott McKenzie wearing flowers in his hair. Apparently, my mental playlist was loaded with Top-10 Odes to San Francisco.

A solitary air-start cart somewhere on the far side of the field, frozen into a snow bank, represented our only chance of getting to California. Our entire escape plan, er . . . I mean departure plan, depended on the mechanic and ramp crew finding it, digging it out and getting it going. I was in awe of their dedication and obvious desire to get rid of us. Meanwhile, we shivered and worked, using our flashlights to find our way, and continued our preparations in hope and faith that our scheme was going to succeed.

Partway through an inspiring rendition of "California Dreaming," Mamma Cass was interrupted by the hulking, winter-dressed mechanic bouncing back into the flight deck. "We got it!" There was a definite smile in his voice. Within minutes the growl of the pneumatic cart roared to life below the flight deck. "Air's ready," a voice called into our headphones. "Okay," Captain Dal said, "let's do this."

I began reading the unfamiliar checklist, speaking loudly over the outside noise. We accomplished each step slowly and deliberately. We couldn't afford any mistakes. We were stepping beyond the standard daily routine. We were going the extra mile to accomplish this departure, but we were also intent upon not damaging our expensive aircraft nor any of the much-more-precious human beings working with us on the ramp.

Gradually needles, gauges and lights flickered on, giving us minimal insight into the aircraft's status. I kept reading checklist items as each of us responded by moving the appropriate switch or confirming a pertinent gauge reading. Then the moment of truth arrived. It was time to hit the Start button. I looked up at the pressure gauge on my panel. "Looks okay—barely," I called out the reading.

"Start number two," Captain Dal commanded. The center engine on top of the fuselage, our number two engine, posed the least risk to the ground crews who were yet to service the plane. As FO Bear held the switch, I watched the start pressure needle drop. "Valve open," I confirmed. The captain was closely monitoring his indicators. They began to move, so slowly. We all stared at the gauges, compelling the engine to spin. "Now or never," Captain Dal muttered, throwing the fuel lever on. There was a short hesitation. Then the exhaust temperature flickered and began climbing. "Light on two," the captain called in a flat tone. His hand stayed on the lever, ready to snap it closed if the temperature climbed too quickly, indicating a misfire inside the engine. The RPM increased sluggishly towards the point where the engine would become self-sustaining. Other parameters crept up slowly. "Forty percent," Captain Dal called out the magic number. Bear released the switch and I glanced up to the pneumatic gauge. "Valve closed," I confirmed.

All our attention turned to our barely-running turbine. It still had to stabilize properly in the frigid winter air or we'd have to shut it down. We glared at the oil pressure reading. My flight deck colleagues were as keen as I to avoid destroying a multi-million-dollar engine. "There we go," FO Bear finally called when a full minute had expired. "Oil Pressure." An air of triumph flooded the flight deck. We were in business! Goodbye warm bed, hello San Francisco. We continued our start procedures. When I flipped on the electrical power, we felt a shudder through the entire plane. The frigid generator kicked into action. It came on-line. It held! More lights, gauges and normal flight deck sounds sparked into action. For the first time that morning, things seemed almost normal. The ramp agent reappeared at the flight deck door, cheeks burning raw from the cold.

"We're in business!" I proclaimed. He grinned back, "Just in time too. The air cart died. We can't get it restarted. This must be your lucky day." My internal eight-track (Hey! This was a long time ago!) burst into a stirring rendition of "California, Here We Come."

As our overhead engine purred away, doing the job its little brother-APU couldn't this morning, we launched into our pre-flight preparations. The flight attendants were soon onboard, organizing the galleys and cabin. The fuel truck was connected and pumping gas. The cabin was not warming up quickly, so we had the passengers don all their winter finery for boarding. As the *purser* closed our cabin door, I glanced back down the aisle and smiled again. One hundred-and-some passengers, wearing parkas and gloves and hats, were all huddled happily in the cold, exchanging smiles and laughter. I imagined the jokes being shared: "These cost-cutting measures have gone too far," and, "I should have flown first class. This economy ticket just wasn't worth freezing my *toes*." (insert appropriate body parts at your discretion).

Then the main door closed and we were ready to push back. The ground crew tractored us off the bridge into the dark morning as I carefully read the 'Cross-Bleed Start' checklist. Using bleed air from number two engine to start the others, we soon had all three jets idling. A draft of warm air poured out of the vents and we were finally back to normal and on our way. The rest of the departure went smoothly. We were all warmed-up and nothing could hold us back. We stopped at Edmonton, then Calgary to load more winter refugees. Soon we were sailing southward along the Rocky Mountains, San Francisco bound. As we descended into **SFO**, the flight culminated with the majestic Point Reyes arrival along the Pacific shores and over a fog-bound Golden Gate bridge.

From the airport, I rented a car and drove to visit my American cousin and her family. We had arranged earlier that I would come spend this layover with them. As I made my way across the hills to Manteca, I felt a lingering sense of satisfaction. Though still a rookie second officer, I had played a significant role this morning in solving an unusual problem. All our crew members, both air and ground-based, had worked together to improvise an unusual departure, everyone contributing their talents, skills and effort.

Throughout my career, I would discover that solving such unexpected problems, often caused by chaotic weather or mechanical failures, was one of the most interesting parts of the job. On these occasions, we humans truly shine. Something in us is made for this—creating solutions to the problems that life and the universe throw at us.

Next morning my cousin plucked a fresh orange from her garden to garnish our breakfast plates. I tried hard not to think about the return flight to Winnipeg.

Note: The coldest-ever recorded temperature in Winnipeg was −47.8 Celsius (−54 Fahrenheit) on December 24, 1879.

10

Tank to the Rescue

✈   ✈   ✈

Second Officer's Log:
1975 / B727 / YWG (Winnipeg) to YYC (Calgary)

I was sitting at the second officer's panel, minding my own business and preparing my system controls for the impending descent into Calgary. The last hour and a half since leaving Winnipeg had been delightfully smooth and routine. The late afternoon sun setting over the Rocky Mountains west of the city flooded the flight deck and all seemed right with the world. This was about to change.

The purser, who'd been around the airline long enough to be on a first name basis with the captain, entered the compartment. She slid beside me to half-sit on the observer's seat where she could directly talk with him.

"Abe, there's a passenger standing in the galley who won't go back to his seat. I need to get things stowed for landing and he's becoming a nuisance. Would one of you "big strong pilots" please come back and take care of it?"

If I'd realized at the time how rarely an experienced flight attendant resorts to calling on the flight deck crew for help with passenger issues, I would have been instantly alerted that she was not just asking a simple thing.

"Has he been drinking? Do you think he could become violent?" Captain Abe asked as he twisted half-around in his seat to make eye contact.

"He's had too much to drink," she said "but no, he's not violent. He just refuses to move and completely ignores my instructions to be seated."

Captain Abe turned to me and said, "Will you go back and see to that? I'll be starting the descent here in about two minutes." He said this last part to emphasize the time constraint. We were closing in on our destination at roughly eight miles a minute and however this got done, it had to be done quickly.

Wait a minute! I wanted to say. *I'm just new on the line and I've never dealt with passengers before. The first officer is more experienced than me. Shouldn't you send him?* You may have heard a similar whine from me before. I became a pilot because pilots get to hide in the flight deck. If I'd wanted to deal with passengers, I'd have become a flight attendant.

"On my way," I answered, trying to sound confident. Standing up, I fastened the top button of my shirt, straightened my tie, put my hat on, but left my blazer hanging in the small flight deck closet. The hat will certainly convey enough stern authority for the situation I thought. I wouldn't want to overwhelm him with my authoritative manner.

I followed the purser out to the forward galley, closing the cockpit door behind me. Stepping into the passenger cabin during flight always gave me an instantaneous attack of cognitive dissonance. It's easy to become isolated in our little flight deck world and forget about all this other stuff following along behind. My mind boggled at the sight of the hundred feet of aisleway extending back, as if forever, and dozens and dozens of passengers peering over the myriad banks of seats. I fleetingly imagined I could see our 727's towering T-tail and the uniquely-embedded center engine rising behind us into the 500-mile-an-hour slipstream. Nothing more than thin aluminum skin sheltered us from the howling wind, many times faster than any hurricane, but here we were going about our business in shirt-sleeve comfort. I blinked and gave my head a mental shake.

The purser nodded towards ***Problematic Passenger (PP)*** to my left. Then she suddenly remembered something important that needed her attention at the back of the plane. Watching her disappear behind the curtain I felt very alone. Problematic Passenger was standing in the galley alcove, his substantial size filling most of the available space. In his right hand, he held a half-empty glass of amber liquid, which rested on his protruding belly. He seemed to be swaying just a little. His shirt sleeves were rolled up, top button open and his expensive tie was askew. I moved carefully into the crowded space to face him. The glaze in his eyes assured me that he was feeling no pain and I mentally scanned the area ensuring the absence of open flames that might ignite his fumes.

"Sir, you have to take your seat now. We'll be landing soon." I tried to use my authoritative big-boy voice. I looked him squarely in the eyes which were at the same level as my own, both of us being over six feet tall. I wanted to make him comply but not to offend him. After all, he was a paying customer. Most of all, as a new employee I was hoping to avoid any potential unpleasantness in my ongoing relationship with my Chief Pilot. I didn't want any letters of complaint from irate passengers appearing on my file. Did I already tell you how I underestimated the significance of an experienced flight attendant asking pilots for help with passenger issues? I should have realized that this person was way past the point of responding to polite requests—even when delivered by a tall authoritative pilot wearing a cool pilot's hat.

"You people do such a good job," he slurred. "I looove flying with you because you make me feel so welcome."

Great, I thought to myself—a friendly drunk. Now it's going to be even harder to get him to sit down without being rude and forceful. I nodded and smiled politely as I raised my voice and repeated my directive. Surely, now he'd comply and move back to his seat. Right?

"Thank you sir. I'm so happy you're enjoying the flight, sir. But sir, you have to get back to your seat now." I tried to sound quite stern. No more mister nice guy. I was going to show him that I meant business. I re-adjusted my hat to draw attention to the awesome authority that I was exuding. I may have even stopped smiling.

He swayed and moved his drink to the other hand as he reached out to shake mine. "You guys do such a good job." He leaned forward, pulling me towards him to punctuate the last word and his shared breath may have put me momentarily over the blood-alcohol limit. I gripped his hand tightly and tried to pull him towards his cabin seat. He planted his feet and became an immovable object to my less than irresistible force. Try as I might I could not get him to acquiesce to my awesome authority.

I pulled my frame to my maximum height as I tried again to coerce him, regretting that I had left my uniform blazer hanging in the flight deck. Surely that would have helped me impress him. I thought briefly about running back to get it. He clasped my hand even more tightly and kept chattering on about what a great airline we were and how much he loved us all.

Then I felt the unmistakable bump of the autopilot disconnecting. Captain Abe was starting the descent. This was confirmed by a chime and the seatbelt signs illuminating—earlier than usual, but probably intended as a signal for me to hurry up. Then I heard the engine power reducing and the rush of interior air flowing as our pressurization system began to adjust to Calgary's altitude. I had set its controls before leaving the flight deck and I needed to get back to continue my pre-landing preparations. I was getting desperate.

My best, most awesome authoritative pleas were having no effect on Problematic Passenger. I was running out of ideas and my training as a pilot had never covered anything like this. I had always assumed that we must always be polite to customers. The only thing I knew about passenger service was the old adage, "the customer is always right." Right? Nervously I scanned the cabin behind me for the purser so I could hand the problem back to her and get back to my flight deck duties, but she was still apparently very busy elsewhere. I could feel the heat building up under my not-so-authoritative hat and a rivulet of sweat ran down my temple. What to do now?

Suddenly, the flight deck door burst open! Intense rays of evening sun blasted from the front windshield down the aisle, outlining the form of First Officer Sherman J. Tyke, affectionately known as "Tank." His tremendous bulk barely fit through the narrow opening. His hatless head barely cleared the transom. His mighty shadow eclipsed the sunlight except for two brilliant beams that radiated like searchlights over his shoulders.

Sherman was probably the largest man I'd ever seen fit into an airliner flight deck. He easily dwarfed every other pilot in the company. His face was round and his voice was low and gravelly. When he smiled, he looked like an iconic Paul Bunyan. But when he frowned, he resembled everyone's nightmare of that person you least want to meet at night in a dark alley. Right now, he was not smiling.

Stomp, stomp, stomp. He moved directly to the galley. "Sir, you have to sit down NOW." Tank clutched PP by the back of his shirt collar and the belt of his pants. To my grateful eyes, it seemed like Tank lifted the large drunken man so his shoes barely touched the carpet. Tank quick-marched him into the cabin towards the first empty seat. He spun the man around like a rag doll, pressed him forcefully into the chair and attached the seatbelt pulling it so tight that I'm sure the man's voice would have gone up an octave if he had still been talking. But he wasn't. The shock and awe of Sherman J. Tyke had totally silenced him.

"AND DON'T GET UP AGAIN UNTIL WE'RE AT THE GATE OR WE'LL CALL THE POLICE!"

With that Tank spun around and clomped back into the flight deck. I trailed along behind like his faithful lap dog. In my imagination, I turned back to wag a finger and add "Yeah! What he said and double!" But in reality, I knew I could add nothing to Tank's impressive performance. I sheepishly followed him back to the pointy end of the plane, closing the door behind and putting away my sadly disgraced hat of authority.

"Everything okay now?" Captain Abe asked. "Just fine," Tank growled. I kept my head down as I rushed to catch up with my descent duties and silently hoped that Tank, or someone like him, would always be there to rescue me. He did not pay for his own beer on our layover that evening.

11

Red Herrings and Strange Noises

✈   ✈   ✈

Second Officer's Log:
Fall 1978 / B727 / YYZ (Toronto) to YWG (Winnipeg)

When I pulled the flight plan from the printer in the dispatch center, I immediately noted the item under *MEL (Minimum Equipment List)/Deferred Maintenance: Number 1 fuel tank quantity indicator unserviceable.* It's just a simple line of coded text, but it meant I was already behind schedule. There were extra duties I needed to accomplish before we could leave. I knew I'd be hard-pressed to get the plane ready for an on-time departure to Winnipeg.

On-time departures are a big deal. Airlines don't like to advertise competitively about safety records because this reminds passengers that accidents happen. If we need to keep convincing them that flying is safe—is it really? So, airlines historically have avoided this tactic and instead crow about more trivial matters, like the entertainment systems and free booze or the lowest ticket prices. *Lowest ticket prices* are rapidly becoming the driving force in the industry, as passengers vote with their dollars for the so-called "Walmartization of every-thing"—the unrelenting drive towards the bottom. Consequently, the best we can accomplish, by working as hard as we do regarding safety, is to have passengers not think about safety at all. Furthermore, our bread-and-butter business travelers, the ones who keep most airlines profitable, place just as much emphasis on schedule as they do on cost.

By any measurement, modern jet transport airplanes have become very safe and highly reliable. They nearly always leave on time and parts hardly ever fall off during flight. The key is redundancy. All the ways in which our aircraft can be broken, yet kept flying, were worked out in advance, during the official certification program. Certification of a new airliner is an extremely expensive, rigorous and legally-binding undertaking. It costs manufacturers millions of dollars to meet

47

all the regulatory requirements before new transport aircraft designs are permitted to carry passengers. When it comes to deciding which malfunctions are acceptable, every conceivable failure is carefully analyzed by the appropriate engineers and experts. Before a less-than-perfect aircraft is allowed to fly and carry passengers, strict cross-checks and limitations are set in place to ensure safety is not compromised. In administering all this, and communicating these required procedures and limitations to flight crews, *MEL* (the Minimum Equipment List) is our guide.

I go to the library and haul the heavy three-ring-binder back to the flight planning counter for a quick conference with the captain and first officer. *MEL* says we are allowed to operate the aircraft until the end of the day only, then it must be fixed. We must apply an alternative method to determine the amount of fuel in the tank. I grimace because the procedure is complex and I haven't done it since my initial training. I'll be doing a "drip check." This is a slightly more elegant version of probing a stick into a tank and seeing how much of the stick comes out wet. It's time-consuming and I don't relish this. We're under constant pressure to stay on schedule and there are several steps involved that could introduce errors. I hurry out to the departure gate, ditch my flight bag in the cockpit and meet the mechanic who's been waiting for me. This procedure requires two people working together because captains get very annoyed about running out of fuel.

We head down the gangway and onto to the ramp. Under the airplane, we are immersed in the half-light of terminal building lights and assailed by the roar of machinery and the frantic activity of tractors and baggage carts and galley trucks and *honey-wagons* and a swarm of people working quickly to get our flight out on time. No one wants to be tagged with causing a delay.

Thankfully, I remembered to bring a flashlight. We have three fuel tanks—one in each wing and a larger one in the center fuselage. I double-check my semi-dyslexic brain to ensure we head towards the correct fuel tank. Number one is in the left wing. The left wing is on the same side as my wristwatch when I face the front of the plane. Hey, I'm the one who's going to have to explain running out of fuel to the captain, mid-flight, while the mechanic is safely at home, tucked in his bed.

We need to find several slotted discs the size of quarters, installed in strategic locations around the bottom of the tank. I'm thankful that the mechanic finds them right away, almost as if he's done this before. One by one, using a screwdriver, he turns and unlocks the slotted heads and pulls down the graduated sticks. They say two heads are better than one. That's only true if we don't copy each other's errors, so we individually read the lines and make sure we agree. At this point, it's just a number. It doesn't tell us yet how much fuel is in the tank. We must consult a complex set of tables stored in the flight deck.

We head back into the plane. As the bridge door slams shut behind us, I'm grateful to escape the unrelenting noise. We thread our way through the line of passengers, who are slowly crowding along the bridge into the cabin, where they are being welcomed by our purser. Inside the cramped flight deck, we take one more set of readings. We need to determine if the airplane is sitting level. Of course, it never is exactly level and this means a further adjustment in our readings. Then we find the correct page, the correct rows and columns for the sticks and numbers we've recorded, and we finally get a number that gives us a quantity. Now I have to convert this quantity to pounds because that's the units JT8D engines burn. It's also how our instruments are calibrated.

I find the slip of paper the fuel truck driver has left on my table, indicating our *uplift*. I convert these units and add them to the fuel recorded in the log from the previous flight. Only when all the numbers square up, are we ready to leave. Phew! This entire procedure has taken about 15 minutes, but it's hectic and distracting and now I have just a few minutes left to accomplish my normal tasks so we can push back on time. Did I mention the importance of on-time departures? Don't worry if you haven't followed all these details—you won't be tested. I just want you to believe me when I say it's complicated and prone to error. (Shortly after this flight, the process became more complicated by the introduction of the metric system in Canada. This was one contributing factor to the infamous Gimli Glider incident, where a B767 ran out of fuel and glided safely to a landing).

Within minutes we're pushing back from the gate into the nighttime darkness of the Toronto ramp. For the duration of the flight, we'll track how much fuel each engine burns and calculate what's still in the tank. The disconcerting thing is that the defunct gauge in the left tank shows twice as much fuel as the one for the right tank. I must ignore this, knowing it's wrong. There's even a strip of maintenance tape installed beside the gauge, reminding me it's to be ignored. But each time I scan the fuel panel, I mentally flinch a little. The apparent discrepancy exceeds the allowable imbalance between the left and right wings. This is an unsafe condition. I have been carefully trained to never, ever create such an imbalance in the fuel because it could compromise control of the aircraft. As much as captains hate running out of fuel, they also hate airplanes that want to *roll* upside down at takeoff. So even though I know the left gauge is inoperative, each time I glance at it, there's a reflexive "yikes!" in my mind, until I remind my mind, not to mind it.

After a quick taxi to the north side of the airport, we roll onto the two-mile-long runway. The first officer who is flying this leg pushes up the power and away we go. I take one last scan of my panels, flinch again at the odd fuel tank readings, then turn my attention to the engine instruments on the front panel. My main task for the duration of the takeoff is to monitor the engine conditions and loudly announce any discrepancies I notice. I remain blissfully silent. We accelerate to our rotation speed. The first officer hauls back on the massive control yoke to start lifting the nose of the heavily-loaded Boeing into the night sky. As he does so, the aircraft tries to *roll* to the left. The first officer compensates by feeding in large amounts of control movement to prevent it. My eyes instinctively go to our fuel load distribution. Did I make a mistake? Is that left fuel tank really over-filled like the gauge is saying? The captain must be thinking the same thing, as I see him glance quickly over his right shoulder, towards the suspect gauge.

"Left wing a little heavy?" he asks the first officer.

"Yeah, but it's fine now..." His control inputs have returned to normal.

We're climbing smartly and the first officer banks the plane into the required departure heading, as he calls for the gear and flap retractions, on schedule. The aircraft handling seems to be normal now. We're busy for the next several minutes, accelerating and reconfiguring the gear and flaps, making the radio frequency changes, following the departure route to intercept our course to Winnipeg and getting subsequent clearances to higher altitudes. But all the while the three of us are wondering about that rolling tendency at lift off. It can't be explained by crosswinds or anything obvious. We're puzzled. We are on the verge of discovering that this fuss about the amount of fuel in the left tank is the least of our problems.

We're through 10,000 feet, the seatbelt sign is switched off and one of our flight attendants suddenly opens the flight deck door. She steps into our darkened domain and asks a question no pilot wants to hear—ever: "What was that terrible, screeching, banging noise during takeoff?"

The captain twists around in his chair, hooking his right arm over the seat back so he can make eye contact with her. "What kind of noise? Where were you sitting? When did it start? Is it still going on?" Quickly we establish that the noise was most apparent at her over-wing seat in the mid cabin. It started partway into the takeoff and suddenly stopped as we became airborne. We're beginning to realize there is something going on other than a fuel imbalance. We get a call from the ATC departure controller: "The flight departing after you saw rubber debris on the runway—maybe from a shredded tire. Your company has been advised and they're sending someone out to take a look."

"Okay, thanks."

We look at one another. We take a quick look around the flight deck control panels. The flaps and gear are all tucked up, everything is working normally. Other than the fuel gauge and the wing drop during lift off—which seems now to be explained by the drag from a failing tire—everything is normal. As we continue climbing en route, our maintenance department calls us on the company frequency to tell us that they found a piece of rubber with a serial number. It is from our left outboard main tire. I'm impressed the records are so precise and accessible that they could figure this out so quickly.

"Well, everything is looking good," the captain replies. He looks at us. "I don't see any problem with continuing, does anyone else?" We shrug and agree. We're already climbing through twenty-five thousand feet and all is well. If nothing else is broken, then why not press on? Our alternative would be to return to Toronto, but before landing, we'd need to dump a considerable amount of fuel and prepare the passengers for a worst-case scenario. Why not do that at a more leisurely pace en route to Winnipeg, rather than compressing it all into a hurried return? Landing at minimal weight with a flat tire isn't the worst thing that can happen to an airliner. The other tire should support our relatively low landing weight; the weather is good and the runway in Winnipeg is just as long as the ones at Toronto.

The captain sends me back for a peek into the visual ports in the floor, to see if there is any damage to the inner tire. I've looked through those ports before. This time the carpet seam is in the correct place, making the task much easier.

"There's not much to see. The inner tire looks fine." More important is what I did not see. "There's no sign of smoke or other damage as far as I can tell." The captain decides—and we all agree—we'll continue to Winnipeg using the three hours along the way to prepare for the landing. He advises our maintenance and dispatch branches of his decision.

The flight progresses routinely. Without rushing, we have time to get out the appropriate checklists to see if they offer any helpful information. *"Land with the aircraft as light as practicable, touchdown as slowly and smoothly as possible and be prepared for pulling towards the bad tire."* It's all pretty obvious. Of course, the worst-case scenarios keep floating through that obsessive-compulsive part of my brain. I push away the mental pictures of losing directional control and careening wildly across the infield, the left wheel showering sparks and bits of rubber. Things like that only happen in simulators—right?

The captain coordinates with our in-charge flight attendant about passenger issues. As a precaution, he wants a full-out emergency landing preparation, where the flight attendants will rehearse the passengers in the heads-down brace position, as well as evacuation procedures. Meanwhile, we have lots of time to discuss the landing amongst ourselves, discussing the potential issues. Almost lost in all these proceedings is the fact that the fuel consumption calculations are working out as expected. There is no issue of fuel imbalance. The tendency for the aircraft to roll at lift off was caused entirely by the drag of the damaged tire.

A few miles before we start our descent, the captain uses the PA to talk to the passengers. Then, following protocol and as planned, he takes control of the plane from the first officer and we begin preparations for descent. The flight attendants follow up with their preparations, which I can hear from the muffled PA announcements behind me. We start our long glide into Winnipeg. We've burned off thousands of pounds of fuel, so we're at a favorable landing weight. The weather in Winnipeg is excellent, with calm winds and clear skies. Everything looks good. We hold our breath for a few seconds when it's time to put the landing gear down, which we do a bit earlier than usual. Three green lights—all good. We've arranged to use the longest runway. The emergency vehicles are standing by. At a thousand feet above the ground, the first officer gives the announcement: "Take position; brace for landing." The touchdown is smooth as silk and as we roll out, the fire trucks follow us down the pavement. I hear a smattering of applause from the passenger cabin. It's all very anti-climactic after the last few hours of anticipation and preparation.

As arranged earlier, once we've stopped on the runway, a company maintenance truck pulls up beside us so a mechanic can inspect the tire. Then we get a call on the inter-phone. "The other tire looks good, Captain. The landing gear pins are installed. You're good to taxi slowly over to the gate." The pins will prevent the landing gear leg collapsing. It's all about an abundance of caution. After we've parked and secured the aircraft and said our goodbyes to the passengers, we three pilots head down to the ramp to see the damage.

It's startling. Worse than I'd imagined. All that remains on the outboard wheel is a ragged casing, with fragments of rubber clinging to shredded strands of the steel belts, which were once embedded in the tire's carcass. The landing gear door is bent where it was flogged by the rotating tire treads as they self-destructed while detaching. Most troubling of all, the engine directly behind the destroyed tire has a large dent on the cowling. It is just an inch below the lip. A chunk of rubber shrapnel had fired back with tremendous force and almost entered the intake. Just a little higher and the engine would have been destroyed. We looked at one another. Only one inch. A little more than the width of a thumb. Such a small distance. That inch made all the difference between our slightly irregular takeoff and a much more dramatic evening.

Several years into the future I would experience another tire failure during takeoff which did destroy the engine. But that's another story.

PART 2
My Own Window
—at Last

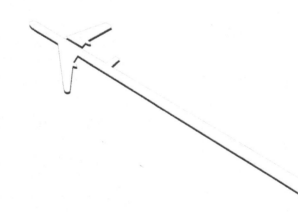

12

By the Numbers

✈   ✈   ✈

Numbers, numbers, numbers. An airline pilot's life is regulated by numbers: show up on time, stay on schedule. The eternal flow of time, expressed as hands sweeping past the ancient twelve daily hours, or glimmering electronic digits, counting away discrete intervals. Either way, time is relentlessly advancing—life is relentlessly slipping away.

Plan your flights by the numbers—fuel, time, altitude, speed. Count the minutes of each flight and watch the fuel number diminish, drawing closer to that fateful moment when the engines will die, whether you're on the ground or in the air.

Maintain altitude within 50 feet, airspeed within five knots, heading within five degrees. Regulate approach speeds, respect flap and landing gear extension speeds. *Fly by the numbers. Land on the numbers.* Arrive on time. Fill in the logbook numbers. Repeat. Repeat. Repeat.

More than anywhere else, pilots' lives are regulated by the numbers of the seniority list. Those numbers determine when we get our chance for promotion in status from second officer to first officer, and on to captain. The seniority list determines the aircraft on which we can hold this status. We are authorized to fly just one type of aircraft at a time—we are specialists. The type of aircraft we fly and our seniority on that type determine which routes we will fly and consequently, the days and number of hours we will work. Our pay-rates are a product of responsibility, productivity and potential liability. Many airlines utilize a formula for pay, based on the hours pilots fly, along with the size and speed of the aircraft. The bigger and faster the aircraft, the higher the pay. Consequently, seniority governs another extremely important number—the amount written on our paychecks.

It took four long years but now, finally, the numbers aligned, like so many stars in an astrological constellation known only to airline pilots. My name, on the annual equipment bid, finally ascended to the DC-9 first officer list. After four years of riding the back seat, taking care of the B727's technical systems and monitoring my colleagues in the front seats, I was now scheduled to begin training as a first officer on the DC-9. After four years, I finally would move into the right-hand front seat—the first officer's chair. I would have my own window!

However, I soon discovered that if I had time to actually look out the window, it was because I had forgotten something I should be doing. The DC-9 first officer's job was generally acknowledged as the busiest in the airline. I would still do almost everything required of me as a B727 second officer, plus I'd be the *PM (Pilot Monitoring)* and *PF (Pilot Flying)* every second leg.

It was time. Another step towards my goal of becoming an airline captain. Uplift.

13

"You Guys Are Going to Kill Me!"

✈ ✈ ✈

"You guys are going to kill me if I'm not careful." Chad Natchel, our DC-9 training captain, was only half-joking.

"You guys are dangerous because you sound like you know what you're doing. The direct-entry pilots don't know all the official company lingo, but they can fly. You guys say all the right things and sound like you know what you're doing, but your flying skills are totally rusty."

Chad was comparing me and my companion-in-training, Raul Bridge, to some of the other DC-9 first officer trainees he had recently worked with.

The airline was entering a period of rapid expansion. In times like this, the company and the pilots' union worked out an arrangement, temporarily permitting outside pilots to be parachuted into spots further up the seniority list, rather than starting at the bottom. This saved re-training them again once everyone settled into their eventual position. It was frustrating for second officers who had been waiting for these flying positions to see direct-entry pilots get trained for these jobs ahead of us. But it was only temporary.

The direct-entry pilots were coming from high-performance business and charter aircraft, regional airlines or the military. Their flying skills were well-honed by many hours of recent practice. We second officers, who had been working for several years as non-flying, third crew-members, were badly out of practice. So, our instructor was only half-joking about our attempts to kill him.

Unhappily, today I was proving his point. My first takeoff in the flight simulator, with an engine cut, turned into a disaster. As we reached the necessary takeoff speed, I began pulling back on the control yoke. The nose rose above the horizon and the view of the runway disappeared. I shifted my eyes to the instruments only to discover that we were already banked crazily towards the left and *rolling* rapidly out of control. The simulator suddenly froze in the midst of crashing as Chad hit the freeze button and repositioned us to the beginning of the runway.

"Okay," he said, "Let's reset and try that again."

It was humiliating to discover how badly my piloting skills had deteriorated. It emphasized for me what I already knew: flying comprises a very perishable set of skills. There is nothing intuitive about flying for us humans. We learn to fly and must keep practicing or we lose it. That is why airline pilots, commercial pilots and even private pilots to some degree, are required to follow very specific *recency rules*. We must fly a specific number of hours and accomplish a minimum number of takeoffs and landings in a specific number of days prior to carrying passengers.

We are also affected negatively by fatigue. When we get tired, our easily-forgotten skills deteriorate. If our gray matter is not fresh and clear, it inevitably shows—we make poor decisions and lose hand-eye-brain coordination. Consequently, pilots are governed by rigorous laws specifying how many hours we fly over specific time-frames.

Toward the end of a long simulator session, our chances of making mistakes increase exponentially as our skills deteriorate through fatigue. But I had no such excuse for my takeoff crash today. We were still in the first hour of training.

Chad reset the simulator and I practiced several more takeoffs with an engine failure at the critical moment. Eventually, I got it right—in fact, I nailed it. By the time of my flight test, my hands and feet reacted instantly—and correctly—to hold the heading within a degree or two. I held the wings level and steady while coaxing the disabled aircraft into a meager climb. Then it was a matter of carefully getting it cleaned up by retracting the landing gear and flaps as we slowly accelerated, finally maneuvering our way around to an accurate single-engine landing.

I passed the flight test in the simulator and my license was duly stamped. By the end of the training, I was happy again. My skills were relearned and upgraded until I could control a DC-9 aircraft through all the required exercises, including irregular and emergency situations. I was back in the groove. Or so I thought.

It was time to head out to the airport for three days of flying circuits in the actual aircraft. Another surprise was in store. While the simulator and most of our company DC-9 fleet consisted of the long-body, Dash-

32 model aircraft, we also had a few rogue aircraft we called "the short nines." These were Dash 15 DC-9s. They featured a different wing configuration and much shorter fuselage, so they exhibited significantly different flying characteristics.

I was suddenly thrown back into learning the basics all over again for this new aircraft type. But now I was clinging to a real aircraft as we gyrated wildly, rolling and yawing on climb-out. I struggled to match the control inputs to the unbalanced forces on the plane as Chad challenged me with one simulated engine failure after another.

I could feel my face turning red with embarrassment as Chad watched from the left seat while I struggled, probably wondering if he'd need to take control and save us from crashing. I was always just a little too late or too early, applying control pressures at the wrong time while the lightly-loaded aircraft shot skyward like a rocket, rolling crazily from right to left. I wonder if the controller watching from his tower kept a hand hovering over the red button, ready to launch the emergency vehicles. Was he expecting us to crash?

Even on one engine, we climbed quickly compared to anything I'd ever flown before. So while my mind was still back on the runway, the airplane was climbing through a thousand feet, and I was already late making power reductions, flap adjustments and turns to new headings. I couldn't keep up.

Over a beer later on, when all the dust had settled and I'd passed the flight checkout in the aircraft, Chad said, "At one point I looked over and was going to offer a suggestion, but I saw the look on your face and figured I'd better not or you might start crying." He wasn't far off. The humiliation an aircraft can produce in a pilot who is out of sync and rapidly "left behind" is like nothing else I can describe. The world is rushing by. My mind-channels are so preoccupied with the speeding flow of events and information that I can't recall what it is I'm supposed to be doing.

This feeling was not new. It was something I discovered at the very beginning of my training as a private pilot. I continually saw it in myself and other pilots throughout our careers. Even the best pilots could easily become overwhelmed by too many things happening, too fast—clinging to the controls, feeling lost and unable to sync our minds and bodies with this metal tube, blasting through the sky!

After the first day's training in the short-nine, I went straight back to my hotel room, deeply dejected. After so many years of waiting to fly an airliner, my dream was being realized. But here I was, having more trouble handling the aircraft than ever before at any level of my training.

As I sat there, I concentrated on a review of the basics. Things I'd learned years ago. I began remembering my way back through the basics of aircraft control. I had to keep reminding myself that I actually knew what to do. It was a matter of getting my hands and feet and brain to do it at the right times, and to stop myself from reacting to the intuitive but incorrect reactions my hands and feet wanted to make before I could sort things out. I was creating what we call **PIOs—pilot induced oscillations**—by being out of sync with the aircraft. I was behind and reacting instead of anticipating and pro-acting.

When an engine quits producing thrust on one side of a multi-engine aircraft, you'd think the airplane would suddenly veer (yaw) towards the dead engine. It does, but due to their design, planes roll more violently while the yaw is hardly detectable. In an airliner with swept wings, the effect is even more pronounced.

When an engine fails, a pilot needs to ignore the instinct to level the wings with his hands on the yoke. Pilots must use the rudder pedals. If we overreact, we overcorrect and the airplane ends up rolling and yawing to the other side, and the startled pilot has to apply corrections in the opposite direction.

Eventually, I learned to apply the right amount of each input, waiting a second or two for the aerodynamic forces to rebalance. Then I could make smaller course corrections while adjusting the nose-up angle, climbing at the required rate, watching our speed and retracting the wheels and wing flaps. It is a challenge. It takes continual practice. It's a perishable skill. This is why we practice "engine cuts" more than all other emergencies.

I got through the DC-9 certification training with the flying instructor still in one piece—though perhaps he sported a few more gray hairs. Then it was time to head out to the line for the next phase of our indoctrination.

14

If I Had It To Do Over

✈ ✈ ✈

First Officer's Log: / DC-9 / YYZ (Toronto) to YQT (Thunder Bay)

I'm riding the crowded jump-seat that folds down across the entrance-door alcove at the rear of the DC-9's dark cockpit. Night has fallen. Just an hour previously, we departed Toronto and turned our backs on its sea of lights. Since then, we have become a strange, ethereal submarine, penetrating an obsidian ocean hiding from us all signs of both the celestial and terrestrial constellations. Thunder Bay, our destination, lies ahead. Tonight, the city sits on the seabed, immersed in wintry storms, sweeping across Northwest Ontario.

Raul Bridges sits immediately ahead and on my right. He is flying this last leg of his en route training regime. Captain Natchel is in the left seat. The flight so far has been smooth. We are at 31,000 feet and the thick clouds surrounding us are benign. Now we're starting our descent towards the western shores of Lake Superior and the howling winter storm below feels malevolent. The landing will be anything but routine.

During the approach briefing, Captain Natchel has advised that due to the challenging conditions in Thunder Bay, and in accordance with our operational restrictions, he will be taking control of the aircraft for the landing. No one is arguing.

Besides the pilot's experience, other factors affect our limits for bad weather landings. For example, on every approach, pilots have to see enough of the runway or its surroundings to either land the aircraft manually or ensure the auto-approach system is guiding us accurately. These visual references are determined by the lights and electronic systems installed on each runway. The busiest airports are equipped with complex and expensive systems, permitting pilots to descend to the lowest possible altitude before the visual references must appear. In such an environment, when the pilots are properly qualified and the aircraft systems are properly functioning, we can descend as low as 50 feet above the runway before deciding to land or go around. Smaller regional airports, like Thunder Bay, have a relatively less complicated, less expensive system, so we must establish our visual cues from a higher altitude.

Tonight we are between the proverbial rock and hard place. The blizzard is howling from the northwest, creating turbulence and white-out conditions. If we choose to land straight ahead, into the wind, we can descend to approximately 600 feet above the runway before we need to establish the visual references. Weather reports say the cloud ceiling is lower than this.

We must approach from the other end of the runway—equipped with a better system of approach aids, including *electronic glide slope* and localizer beams, as well as brighter lights, allowing us to descend to 200 feet. For that runway, we'll be flying with a quartering tailwind. It is gusting near the limits of what is legal—and sensible.

Furthermore, we've received reports that the dark asphalt runway is coated in slush and snow. The sweeper truck has been working steadily since the storm began several hours ago, but it can't keep up. The conditions are changing rapidly. This is definitely not a night for a newly-trained first officer to be practicing his landings.

Throughout this approach, Captain Natchel must continually discern whether the total picture—the approach aids, the visibility, wind and runway conditions and piloting experience—meets the required safety standards. If any of this becomes doubtful, he'll immediately cancel the approach and divert to our alternate airport. However, his judgment can only be as good as the information we have.

Descending, sinking through layers of clouds, we carve around the north side of the airport, jolting roughly against our seatbelts. We are encountering turbulence caused by surface winds deflecting off the rugged hills surrounding the airport. Raul is working hard. The front windshield and wiper blades are accumulating ice, revealed by Captain Natchel's probing flashlight beam. He has switched on our wing and engine de-icing systems. Now Raul needs to keep the engines running at a higher power setting to guarantee enough hot air to melt this ice and prevent more from forming.

Raul needs more drag to counteract. He reaches to the center console and extends the wing-mounted speed brakes. He calls for the flaps and landing gear earlier than usual. Captain Natchel moves for the appropriate controls, makes the required confirmations and calls them out. Raul's struggles are a little like driving a car on ice—keeping one foot on the brake and the other one on the gas to keep the engine from stalling, while negotiating an obstacle course that can't be seen, but only discerned from the flickering needles encased in pools of light on the dark instrument panel. As our salty old Chief Pilot has been known to say: "Hey, that's why you guys make the big bucks."

As we turn back into the eastbound approach path, things get worse. The tailwind blows us more rapidly over the ground towards the airport. Raul is doing a good job but as the glide slope and localizer needles swing into view and stabilize on the dials, the captain moves his hands and feet into position, and calls: "I have control."

He speaks loudly, to be heard over the flight deck noises. Raul seems happy to release his grip and switch to his **PM** (pilot monitoring) duties. He grabs the microphone and reports to ATC that we are now established on final approach.

The radar controller, located somewhere far away, watches our electronic blip on a pulsing screen, gives us the frequency for the Thunder Bay control tower and tells us to switch over. The tower controller will be able to give us landing clearance and updates on the weather and runway conditions.

The aircraft is constantly rocking and thumping, the tailwind causing the groundspeed to stay higher than we'd like. Natchel has us locked onto the electronic guidance.

A needle on the panel flickers and swings to point in the other direction. We've crossed the **YQT** (Thunder Bay Airport) beacon. Raul obtains the latest wind report from the tower and confirms our landing clearance. From my perch at the back of the flight deck, the world outside our front windows is pitch black, punctuated with red flashes from our rotating beacon, strobing off the dense clouds.

Captain Natchel is busily working the controls. He keeps the *ILS (Instrument Landing System)* needles centered, tracking the electronic signals. The airspeed is on target but fluctuating with each gust of wind. The wings rock abruptly from side to side, but never too far away from center before he catches them. Then with the next gust, he re-levels them.

The altimeter is winding down, towards the ***DH (Decision Height).*** The lighted instrument pools in the dark cockpit panels mesmerize as they quietly tell their story. I blink to keep alert and remind myself the information they communicate is a little terrifying. We are strapped inside an aluminum tube, sinking into the teeth of a wild winter storm, at a hundred and fifty miles per hour. We are descending over primeval forests, rocks and wilderness, towards a narrow black strip—snow- and ice-covered asphalt.

We may or may not be able to see that asphalt at the critical moment, when the captain must decide to land or go around. As long as everything he does remains tightly bound by the parameters and limitations to which this approach system is designed, and so long as the thousands of complex pieces and components of the airplane keep functioning correctly, he might succeed in accurately reuniting this projectile with the earth. Hopefully, that will be within the barely-wide-enough first thousand feet or so of the runway, leaving us barely-adequate room to stop.

If any of a dozen different things that can go wrong does go wrong, we will be unable to land and could suddenly come closer to disaster than anyone ever hoped. Yet we have all signed on for this because it works out—most of the time. Airlines manage to keep their kill-rates below the acceptable standards—most of the time. After all, we want the passengers to keep showing up, buying tickets and keeping the whole system going.

"One hundred above," Raul calls, breaking into my distracted thoughts.

"Roger," the captain acknowledges.

The front windshield remains mostly black, but I think I catch a small glimpse of a ground light as it slides beneath the nose. Our altitude keeps winding down. A dim yellow annunciator light suddenly illuminates, then goes out, and the hand on the radar altimeter jumps up and down, tracing the unevenness of the rocky ground below. The main altimeter needle continues down and aligns with the white plastic bug—the minimum descent altitude. Now the yellow radar altimeter light comes on steadily and stays on. We are at the "now or never" point.

"Minimum!" Raul calls, "I have some approach lights."

"Continue..." the captain answers. "Give me the landing lights."

Raul reaches to the overhead panel and flips two large switches. The outside lights suddenly flare, illuminating puffs of wet gray clouds slashing past our windows. More ground lights and then some runway threshold lights come into view.

"Runway in sight!"

"Landing. Wipers full."

The front windows are soaked in melted snow and more is accumulating as we plow through a horizontal tornado of snowflake-asteroids. It's all like a scene from a Star Wars movie. The rubber blades, stowed along the bottom of the windshield, noisily begin sweeping and slapping away at the water and accumulated slush. The racket almost drowns out all other flight deck noise.

Looking over the nose of the plane, I see the thin, dim, yellow strand of approach lights sliding beneath us. They are materializing, one by one, from the murky clouds ahead. Then, another line of green lights emerges and crosses our path at a right angle, marking the beginning of the runway. Beyond that, a dark oblivion where the runway is supposed to be. I've seen this view before. I accept, as an act of faith, that the blackness really is our runway.

For a moment, it seems we are about to descend into a black, bottomless pit. The darkness absorbs the landing lights, revealing nothing. Then, faint details of paint, skid marks and tracks in the slush and snow appear beneath us. We swoop over the runway threshold, which creates an overwhelming sense of how fast we are rushing headlong toward the far end of this finite strip of pavement. The tailwind is propelling us along, too fast for this short runway. My breath catches.

Captain Natchel obviously has the same impression because he makes no effort to flare. We hit the pavement solidly—but there's no sensation of sudden drag from the wheels. Surface friction is marginal. The captain calls for Raul to deploy the reversers while he quickly yanks back the spoiler lever. The reversers roar to life. We feel the spoiler panels thrust upwards from the wing's surface, dropping the full weight of the airframe onto the landing gear. Natchel carefully plants the nosewheel into the slush-covered surface, then slides his feet up the pedals to tromp the brakes while pulling the reverse levers back as far as they will go.

Noise from the DC-9's rear-mounted engines, nearly a hundred feet behind us, seldom penetrates the flight deck. But tonight we hear a rising, dull roar. We decelerate, but too gradually, and Natchel pulls back harder, keeping the levers against the stops. The roar envelopes us and grows louder.

Our airspeed is decreasing—but so slowly! The captain's left hand continuously holds the yoke against the crosswind. From my vantage point, I can see his knees moving. His feet are rapidly working the rudder pedals, keeping us in the middle of the runway, aligned with the center line. He keeps the brake pedals fully depressed so the anti-skid system will give us as much braking as the tires can grab against the slippery surface.

Outside, I can barely see parallel strips of lights along the edges of the pavement rushing by, almost blurring. But the rate is slowing, very gradually. Whether or not we are going to stop within the available length of the runway is still in doubt. It is obvious the braking-action reports we'd received earlier were outdated and inaccurate.

During briefing for the approach, many minutes before, we looked up the runway length needed to land in these conditions. These numbers assured us the Thunder Bay runway would be adequate—barely. However, slush, snow and ice introduce variables beyond our ability to predict. We can only make the appropriate corrections, using the appropriate values, and hope the built-in buffers will be adequate. There is a lot of carefully-engineered, scientific theory built into our procedures. However, the chaos of reality sometimes refuses to comply with the finest theories.

This uncomfortable refusal of reality to conform to procedures is acknowledged in our documents. Pilots call these *CYA ("cover your ass")* statements. The governing authorities relieve themselves from complicity by writing something like, "These charts and tables provide guidance only. Final responsibility, for safe operation, rests with the pilot in command."

In the end, it always comes down to an experienced human pilot, who has hopefully been here before, making an on-the-spot-assessment based upon the best—but imperfect—information available. We live in a chaotic universe. Fuzzy human logic, honed by thousands of hours of practice, is often all we have left to rely on.

So when Raul makes his call, "70 knots," which normally signals the pilot handling the airplane to reduce the thrust reversers to idle, Captain Natchel does not. He keeps them at full power. Neither Raul nor I are surprised. We all see the end of the runway emerging from the gloom—and dim lights ahead.

Now the roar of the engines grows incessantly louder. The reason we normally return the engines to forward-thrust by now is to avoid what happens next. We begin hearing the loud "pop–thud–pop" sounds from the turbulent engine exhaust, recirculating and being sucked in by the engines again. This recycled air causes the engines to backfire with what are termed compressor stalls. They are loud and disconcerting, especially for nervous passengers, but seldom do they actually damage the engines.

The forward momentum of the airplane slowly diminishes. With only a couple hundred feet of pavement between us and the red lights marking the end of the runway, we stop. Natchel returns the thrust levers to the idle positions. He relaxes his toehold on the brake pedals—just a little. Now he can release the yoke and switch his left hand to the tiller, swinging us over to the left side of the runway and sweeping the aircraft's heading around to the opposite direction. We creep back slowly to the exit point.

As we turn off the runway and into the deeply slush-covered taxiways and ramp, we are all quiet. "Well, wasn't that interesting?" the captain finally mutters. Then he calls, "After-landing check," and Raul begins the drill, moving items and chanting the required words out loud. Returning to familiar activity relieves the tension. The atmosphere in our flight deck regains a sense of normalcy. Raul clicks his mic button and tells the tower controller when we're clear of the runway.

The controller says, "There's another company aircraft inbound. He's asking for your comments about the approach."

Pilots help one another, filing what we call *PIREPS (pilot reports)* for all other aviators, regardless of airline affiliation. There are times and circumstances where professional loyalties transcend company rivalries. Tonight, this is one of our own colleagues asking about what to expect when they arrive here.

This is probably the reason Captain Natchel goes beyond the typical factual format for such reports. Usually, we might say what kind of wind and turbulence we encountered, followed by the visibility and altitude at which we acquired sight of the runway. Then we might throw in an official comment about the braking action using terms like fair, poor or even nil. But tonight, Natchel summarizes all this in a succinct and telling comment, designed to convey a warning, without revealing anything on the public airways or ATC recordings that might be misconstrued.

He keys his microphone. "Well, let me put it this way. If I had it to do over again—I wouldn't bother."

There is only a short silence on the frequency, then the incoming flight crew requests from ATC, a re-clearance to divert back to their departure airport. They got the point.

Meanwhile, we pull into our gate, arriving on schedule. Another routine, if somewhat bumpy flight as far as our passengers are concerned. They're happy to arrive, and as we cross through the crowd inside the terminal, we see people enthusiastically greeting one another: "We weren't sure you'd make it! We almost got stuck on the highway, driving here."

We make our way out to the taxi stand to find our hotel shuttle-bus waiting. The pilots become passengers. Our driver skillfully delivers us safely through the storm to our night layover. Another day's work, finished—the inevitable surprises handled.

15

Sudbury Four Footed Shuffle

✈ ✈ ✈

*"Who's driving this thing?" and the importance of
communication, humility and grace in the recovery.*

First Officer's Log:
1979 / DC-9 / YQT (Thunder Bay) to YSB (Sudbury)

Captain Blue was a gentleman and an excellent hands-and-feet pilot. His military career culminated with a tour as the solo performer for the nation's air demonstration team. They don't let just anyone do that. But when he moved from single pilot fighter jets to airliners, Blue never seemed comfortable sharing the cockpit. He would let his first officers fly every other leg as expected, but he'd seldom involve us in the flight-management decisions, such as which runway to use or which flap and thrust settings might work best in each situation.

Blue also varied from the company **SOPs** (Standard Operating Procedures) in some small ways that were uniquely his own. Because of this, I was unwittingly set up for an embarrassing lesson in why SOPs are important for the safe operation of airliners.

Here's what happened. Stay with me for this explanation; it gets a little technical.

Pilots have two basic tools for slowing the airplane after landing. First and foremost, we have brakes which we operate using the same pedals that control the rudder and nosewheel. The left foot works the brakes on the left wheel and the right foot works the brakes on the right wheel. To help the tires grip more and skid less we also extend spoilers on top of the wings to ruin *lift* and transfer the airplane's weight onto the landing gear.

Second, we have thrust reversers. The airflow jetting out the back of the engine is redirected by a system of deflectors and valves to produce negative thrust. This is helpful on slippery runways, but it comes with a certain risk. If the reversers deploy asymmetrically or one fails altogether, the aircraft could be pulled suddenly toward the edge of the runway. Running off the pavement, making big ruts in the infield grass, wiping out some runway lights and damaging the tires is considered *A Very Bad Thing*.

To reduce these risks many airlines divide the workload after landing between the (PF) pilot flying and the (PM) pilot monitoring. The PM opens the reverse thrusters and ensures both are operating evenly before transferring control of these levers to the PF. The pilot flying then adds more power if desired or cancels the reverse thrust as the speed diminishes.

Roll-out is a complex maneuver and takes a few practice runs in the simulator to get it all working smoothly, with proper coordination between the two pilots. It involves moving the control yoke after touchdown to gently lower the nosewheel while balancing the wings against crosswinds. Meanwhile, we are steering with our feet to stay in the middle of the runway. Finally, we apply brakes and thrust reversers to stop.

When the aircraft is ready to exit the runway, the captain must resume control because only the captain on the DC-9 has a tiller for making sharper turns at slow speeds. I suspect that it was designed this way because captains hate talking on the radio at busy airports and can't be bothered memorizing all the various frequencies and taxi routes that the ground controller may assign. It may also save weight and complexity but I like my story better.

Now if you followed the gist of these activities after landing, let me explain how Blue did things his own way.

The SOPs called for the first officer to finish the landing using the brakes and reverse thrusters to bring the airplane close to taxi speed at which point the captain resumed control. Blue, however, would take control immediately after touchdown while we were still rolling at high speed. I came to think of it as *"landus interruptus."* Unfinished business.

For an entire month, I'd flown exclusively with Captain Blue. This involved approximately sixty to eighty landings, half of which I'd flown so I was now fully re-trained to his way. Blue's *"after sequence"* went like this: I'd land the aircraft, close the thrust levers and call for the reversers. Captain Blue would confirm spoiler extension and pull out the reverse levers calling, "Spoilers Up, Reverse Deployed, I Have Control..." all in one quick sentence. Remember this sentence. It plays a key role in how I am soon to mess up. You'll be tested later.

The phrase, "I have control," is an internationally standardized call. The transfer of control of a speeding aircraft must never be in doubt. It was my signal to release the yoke and slide my feet off the rudder pedals while Blue finished the landing. So as soon as Blue said this key phrase, I was finished with my part even though we were still moving along the pavement at a high rate of knots. So, thanks to this re-programming, I am now a bad surprise waiting to happen to the next unsuspecting captain who would fly with me. That happens to be Captain Leroy.

It's a new month and Leroy has drawn the short straw (me). He doesn't realize he's been set up. A couple of months ago soon after finishing my DC-9 upgrade course, I'd flown with him briefly and things must have gone okay because he's not treating me like a potential hazard. I'm about to change this.

The day starts out well enough. Leroy flies the first leg from Winnipeg to Thunder Bay. Nice weather, routine trip, so far, so good. Now as he taxies the little Douglas DC-9 airliner onto the runway at Thunder Bay for our second leg to Sudbury, Captain Leroy is not expecting any bad surprises. As usual, he tells me when to take over by saying, "You have control." And when Captain Leroy says you have control, he really means it. He expects me to manage the flight profile efficiently as well as fly the plane. And this morning the trip over to Sudbury goes well.

Before descending, I tell Leroy that I plan to use the full fifty degrees of landing flaps to help us make the most convenient turnoff. That's at an intersection two-thirds of the way down the runway. His silent nod means he concurs. I sound like I know what I am doing. I am lulling him into a false sense of security. My planning is accurate, resulting in a smooth gliding descent down to the final approach for runway zero-four. As we *"turn final,"* I call for the "Before Landing Check" and the *final flap setting* and Leroy carries out my requests. All seems right with the world—for now.

We touch down nicely within the first thousand feet of runway. I pull the throttles back to idle, calling for "Reverse" and Captain Leroy reaches up and does the usual yanking and makes the usual calls: "Spoilers up; Reverse deployed." I fail to notice what he does not call. Did you notice what he did not call? He does not call out the coded phrase, "I have control." My failure to notice is a critical oversight because I am now busy doing what I've learned to do in my previous landings with Blue—which is nothing. For several seconds, we both sit waiting for the other to apply the brakes. And the runway continues to roll by. Reverse thrust and spoilers alone will not stop a DC-9 within the confines of the Sudbury runway. Ask me how I know.

As the exit point rapidly approaches, we both suddenly realize what's not happening and we both snap into action. "Brakes!" And we both simultaneously stomp the pedals with our size twelves. Now Leroy calls, "I have control!" but it is too late to avoid that one long second or two when the brakes grab fiercely, causing a lurching dive of the nose. "Sorry!" I call, "You have control!" as I pull my feet back from the pedals.

We decelerate rapidly and Leroy does a one-hundred and eighty degree turn to come back to our missed exit. No real harm done except for a shattered ego on my part and sudden, but only temporary, cardiac arrest on Captain Leroy's part. I think he'll look even more distinguished now with that extra gray hair. But who knows what damage the sudden lurch has caused to a nervous passenger's undergarments? I apologize profusely while feeling confused and embarrassed.

I am so discombobulated by that screw-up that I forget to switch the radio to the Sudbury ground control frequency until Leroy reminds me. In my confusion about the first mistake, I compound the situation by making another. I force myself to settle down and concentrate on the job at hand. It is only later, after we are safely parked at the loading bridge, that I figure out why I "fell asleep" at the wheel—why I stopped controlling the airplane before Leroy took over. I figure out how my flights with Captain Blue had inadvertently re-trained me. That's my story and I'm sticking to it.

I don't remember exactly what else happened the rest of that day. I do recall that Leroy assigned me to stand at the flight deck door that chilly morning in Sudbury to say 'goodbye' to our passengers. I smiled at them reassuringly while mumbling something about "a small braking issue." I hope it didn't alarm you." At least not as much as it did me!

I also remember that Leroy invoked the standard captain's slap-on-the-wrist for unsatisfactory performance in a first officer. He did not share flying legs with me for the remainder of that day—and maybe the next. However, when he did once again give me control just before takeoff, he included a slightly sarcastic reminder: "You'll recall that the brake controls on this DC-9 aircraft are situated on the tops of the rudder pedals."

Over the years, the aviation industry has placed increasing emphasis on Standard Operating Procedures (SOPs) and proper crew briefings. These briefings are expected to cover many items—including the point at which the captain will take back control of the aircraft after landing. Good idea.

Excerpt from a modern flight standards document:

Briefings: *Pilots will use clear and concise briefings through the various phases of flight to ensure that the entire crew is informed of the course of action to be taken. Standard briefings formats will be used and all required information will be discussed.*

16

Finding Center:
The Discontented Pilot

✈   ✈   ✈

First Officer's Log:
1980 / DC-9 / YWG (Winnipeg) taxiing out

"You know, this job isn't fun anymore. It's so routine. Some captains drive me crazy with their idiosyncrasies and inefficient practices. When I try to show them a better idea, they don't listen. In fact, they get ticked off with me." I could hear the discontent loud and clear from First Officer Tommy Turrel. *"It'll be better when I get promoted to captain,"* he said. *"Then I'll be able to run things my way and it'll be fun again."*

Tom confided his frustrations to me several years before when we were crew members together on the B727. He was first officer and I was second officer. Since then we've both advanced a notch. Today we're working together for the first time on the DC-9. We are taxiing towards the far runway so we have a couple of moments to chat. Tommy now has his coveted captain's job. He sits in the left seat. I sit to his right as first officer, still getting comfortable with my new role.

"How are you enjoying the captain's seat?" I ask.

"You know, it's still the same job," he says. He sounds disappointed. "I thought that once I upgraded to captain I'd enjoy it more, but it's still the same." His reply surprises me.

I learned something important from Tommy that day. No matter how much I enjoy flying, I realized I'd better look for something deeper than a job on which to center my life. I should seek something that does not depend upon my employment status.

This is a realization some pilots come to, while others never do. They remain forever focused on moving up the seniority ladder, always certain that the next promotion will bring the 'fun' back into life. Eventually, the same ennui, the same listlessness and lack of excitement returns. Consequently, when the airline industry takes a nosedive, which it always does at regular intervals, pilots are understandably shaken. As career advancement stagnates we can experience frustration and even anger.

Meanwhile, pilots who have centered themselves elsewhere recognize the current troubles, but still manage to enjoy the wonders of life.

Another colleague put it this way one day during our initial training days together. "I just realized my whole life is now mapped out! I'll be a Boeing 727 second officer, then a DC-9 first officer, then a B-767 first officer, then a DC-9 captain, then a 727 captain, then a 767 captain. I'll never make it to the left seat of the Boeing 747 because I'm too old. The only pilots who'll ever gain enough seniority to fly the left seat of the B747 are the ones who are hired when they're eighteen... So, I'll remain a B-767 captain until I retire. Then I'll die."

He was obviously discontented by this prospect. He began looking for excitement beyond his career. It wasn't long before stories emerged about debts he had piled up from stock market losses. These were soon followed by stories of gambling problems. Within a few years, he left the airline altogether. He was still searching for something that could not be fulfilled by a career.

I think we all get like that at some point in our lives. When this happens, it's critical that we zero in on the true source of our discontentment so we might find a real solution, rather than repeating the same pattern. For example, I've seen colleagues struggle through divorce but then remarry—a younger version of the same wife. Before long they'd confide over a beer on layovers that the new marriage was suffering from similar problems they'd had in the first one.

After that conversation with Tommy Turrell, I wondered how I would deal with my own issues as the job gradually became more and more routine—as all jobs do. What I couldn't know was that a day would arrive when I would be forced to search even more urgently for "the meaning of life" and the role my career plays in this—all due to a simple blip on an *EKG* test during a recurrent medical examination.

17

LAS1 All Night Long

✈ ✈ ✈

**First Officer's Log:
November 1984 / DC-9 /
YWG (Winnipeg) to LAS (Las Vegas)**

"Have I shown you how I can blow smoke out of my eyes?"

Now that's something that belongs on my list of "things I never expected to hear." I worked with many interesting characters over the years. Cary Swager, affectionately known as Old Smokey in my imagination, was one of them. I got to know him a lot better thanks to one November's unfortunate schedule.

Working conditions, like most things at a large airline, depend on seniority. The longer we've been around and the higher we are up the list, the more choices we have of flights, days off, vacation times and so on. Each month we submit a bid specifying our preferences. Once, I lost track of the deadline and forgot to bid. Consequently, the following month my schedule was comprised entirely of overnight charters to Las Vegas that no one else wanted. I was not pleased. By the way, this was the first and last time I ever forgot to bid.

I'm flying all these trips with the same captain—Cary "Smokey" Swager. I'm not sure what he did wrong to be assigned these flights. As his nickname suggests, he's a chain smoker. The DC-9 cockpit is small. The ventilation is barely adequate at the best of times. I'm sensitive to cigarette smoke. This is going to be a long, hard month. I'm feeling grumpy before we even begin our first trip. I've been rehearsing ways to ask him about keeping the smoke to himself. It's a delicate topic. After all, he's the captain. It's his ship. I really (at that time in history at least) have little recourse.

My worst days of having to share the flight deck with heavy smokers were back when I was still a B727 second officer. I would cringe whenever I found myself scheduled for an entire month with a particularly heavy-smoking captain and first officer duo. They both loved to puff on big stogies that filled our tiny cabin with stenches of bluish smoke. After a day's work with those characters, I'd jump into a shower to wash the stink off my skin and hair, wishing I could just burn my uniform. By the late 1980s, airlines began instituting a ban on smoking in the passenger cabin while still allowing it in the cockpit. But friction was building among pilots, as adamant non-smokers refused to remain in the confined flight deck while other pilots lit up. There were stories of pilots almost coming to blows. It was a great day for me and other non-smoking pilots when finally, in the 1990s, smoking bans spread to most airlines, including the flight decks.

But this November in 1984, smoking is not prohibited and I need to deal with it. Consequently, tonight is truth telling time. This flight will set the tone for the entire month. If I just ignore my issues with the smoke, then I will have to endure an entire month of all-nighter flights bathed in toxic fumes. If I broach the topic but do it awkwardly, how will Captain Smokey respond? Will it make for a longer, tougher month of ill-will between us?

Night has fallen on this wintry day in Winnipeg. We finish our flight planning and on the way to our gate, we stop by the coffee shop for a hit of caffeine. Our schedule calls for a 9 pm departure, flying for three hours, then landing at Las Vegas at 10 pm their time (a two-hour time zone difference). Then we cool our heels for a few hours, leave Las Vegas at 1 am and arrive in Winnipeg at 6 am. Not my favorite hours for working.

As we leave the coffee shop, I take a deep breath and broach the topic. "Hey Cary," I say. "I have a favor to ask." He glances my way as we keep walking. "I'm kind of sensitive to cigarette smoke. I know the Nine's flight deck is pretty confined and there's only so much you can do, but if there's any way you can keep the smoke from drifting my way during the trip, I'd sure appreciate it."

Long pause. Is he ticked off?

Finally, he gives me the old side-eye glance, and in his gravelly smoker's voice, mutters something along the lines, "Well, since you asked nicely, I'll see what I can do." Cary has a reputation of being a strong-willed character and some of the first officers have trouble flying with him because of it. The tone of his voice seems sincere, but he's hard to read. I decide to take his response as a positive sign.

Soon we are airborne, climbing into the night with our cabin full of Vegas-bound gamblers. At cruise altitude, the sky is brilliant with stars and there are faint waves of winter auroras to the north. The dark pools of prairie fields below are outlined by fainter earth-based constellations indicating small towns, roads and farmers' homes. We've just completed our top of climb fuel check, our initial estimates for arrival time and signed on with the American ATC controllers. Smokey rummages into his shirt pocket to pull out his pack of cigs and lights up. I open my fresh air nozzle and point it along the outside wall, hoping it will entrain smoke away from my face.

He takes his first drag and then turns his face away from me, towards his outside wall to exhale. He is holding his cigarette next to his own fresh air nozzle so the smoke from the smoldering cylinder will flow back to the rear of the cockpit and hopefully, out the exhaust vents. "Does this help?" he asks and he's sincere. I assure him it does. It's far from perfect but still much better than it might be otherwise. I'm grateful.

"I like that you asked politely," he says after a few minutes. "When some guys get rude or demanding, I hold the cigarette in my right hand while I tap on the gauge to check the pressurization system." He lifts his empty right hand across the cockpit to the overhead panel just above my head and gently taps on a small round dial. It jiggles a bit and settles into a more accurate reading. The PM (pilot monitoring) normally does this every five thousand feet during our climbs and descents. "I make sure the ashes fall all over his pant leg." He giggles a little and grins. "You'd be surprised how much that pisses people off."

I find his boyish grin and dark sense of humor disarming. I decide I like him and I'm glad I didn't get myself into his bad books. Mama always said I'd get further in life using honey instead of vinegar.

But this news has aroused my curiosity. For the next several weeks I will surreptitiously look for first officers with burn marks on their left pant legs. I never find any, so then I wonder if Cary was just pulling my leg a little. His dry sense of humor was not always easy to read. We all fantasize about rude things we'd like to do to people who disrespect us, don't we? Or is it just me?

That's when he says, "Hey, have I shown you how I can blow smoke out my eyes?" I wonder if I misheard which end of his anatomy is involved, but before I can ask him to repeat himself, he pinches his nose, clamps his mouth shut and sure enough, a pair of smoke-streams shoot from the corners of his eyeballs, swirling into the bright pools of the overhead map lights in the dim cockpit. It's kind of impressive—and disturbing.

"Whoa!"

"Was in a car accident when I was younger. Smashed my face up pretty badly. I guess they couldn't get all the pieces back together. Or maybe I really do have a few screws loose." Now the crooked smile and asymmetry of his thin face begin to connect to Cary's little-known past. *We are all a walking library of stories, many of them painful and tragic.* Mostly, they remain untold, known only to ourselves. I like this self-deprecating twist in his humor and laugh briefly out loud. The upcoming month of overnight flying suddenly seems less daunting.

Several minutes pass in silence. The night grows deeper and quieter still as fewer aircraft are talking on the radio. The air is smooth and except for the glowing dials assuring me otherwise, we might be frozen in time and space.

Cary reaches around the panels and turns down the intensity of the lights on his side of the flight deck to almost nothing. He asks me to do the same. We've been tracking west across the USA, where the lower ground-bound constellations have faded out. Populated regions have given way to arid wilderness. But overhead, the vast, deep, black, star-filled sky becomes more overwhelming as our eyes adjust to the dark. I've heard the night sky described as a cathedral before, but suddenly this takes on new meaning. This is awe-inspiring beyond any earthbound experience.

Cary pulls his chair as far forward as it goes so his face is almost touching the heated windshield. Inside, calmness, serenity, awe. Outside, just inches from his nose, a 500 mph blast howls with the power to tear us to shreds. But here inside, it's easy to deny that we are moving at all.

"I'm determined to see a UFO before I retire."

There's a new revelation. If ever anyone wanted a perfect UFO observation platform, we have it.

"Ever seen one?" I ask.

"Not yet. Plenty of falling stars. And satellites. But no UFOs yet. But one day..."

I pull my chair closer to the window as well. I wouldn't want to miss out if this is the night he finally sees one. I smile to myself. "What do you think are the chances?"

"Who knows," he says. "I just can't believe there's no one else out there in all that space, among all those stars and planets."

I ponder that for a bit. I have never been able to form a strong opinion, one way or another about the existence of ETs. I listen to one scientist explain why it's almost certain and believe him for a while. Then I hear another argue why it's highly unlikely and find myself believing that too. I guess I'll have to withhold judgment for now. Until it happens, I'll never know for sure.

The night progresses slowly. The passage of time and distance is marked only by the rotation of the night sky constellations above, the slow creep of scattered earthbound constellations below and the need to talk briefly on the radio as we transit from one air traffic control frequency to the next. I eventually face a more important question than the existence of other beings in the universe. Namely, how do I keep my own being from falling asleep? The quiet of the night, the lack of activity, the steady whoosh of the air-conditioning system and the low rush of wind on the windows are all combining into a white noise that every now and then threatens to fade out. I force myself to move and stretch and open my eyes as wide as possible, triggering a big yawn.

At times like this, it's a good idea to get up and move around. We may be surrounded by unlimited space but the Douglas designers didn't bother to encapsulate much of it into the DC-9 flight deck. I am barely able to stand to my full height by squeezing back into the small alcove where the bi-fold cabin door swings open. I move and stretch as much as I can, hoping a hurried flight attendant doesn't suddenly fling the door open, nailing me with the hinge right between the shoulder blades.

I'm getting suspicious that aircraft designers think of pilots as just a nuisance. We take up valuable floor space that could be used for so many better things—like cramming in more passengers. I've heard some old timer pilots talk wistfully about the Vickers Vanguard. Its flight deck was so wide pilots could get in and out of their seats along the outside wall. I contrast this to the way we now have to crouch and half hurdle over the center console, hoping to avoid knocking ourselves unconscious against the sloping roofline. The acrobatics are so daunting, especially for taller pilots, I'm surprised there haven't been more incidents of pilots accidentally bumping the flight controls. One more reason for passengers to keep their belts fastened. After a couple of minutes, I ask Cary if he wants anything from the galley, then I slip out to the passenger cabin. I open and close the door as quickly as I can to limit the light penetrating the cockpit and save his night vision. Our flight attendant crew has finished most of their service by now, so someone helps me find our crew snacks and a couple of cups of coffee. Gathering these I retreat to the dark cockpit recesses.

We eat our snacks in quietness and pass the rest of the flight absorbed with our routine tasks. Fuel checks: good. Winds and ground speed: as forecast. Air: smooth. **ETA:** still good. Aircraft systems: all good. I radio reports to our company at required intervals. I continue listening and responding to the infrequent calls from ATC and change frequencies as directed.

Eventually, Las Vegas materializes ahead of us at the seam where earth meets sky. It's startling how far we can see to the horizon on a clear night. The countless lights beaming into the surrounding dark make Las Vegas seem exaggerated, larger than life. As we draw nearer, the city reluctantly reveals its true dimensions. It's not as large as the brightness claims. At first, I imagine I'm looking at a city the size of New York or Los Angeles. Instead, I eventually see an overgrown desert town of maybe half a million people. I'm a little disappointed. Apparently, not everyone who comes to Las Vegas stays in Las Vegas.

We get busy again. The activity feels good. Soon I'm wide awake as we slide gently down the glide path into McCarran Field's long asphalt runways. Cary guides us into the pool of bright runway rushing under us, revealed in the long beams of our landing lights. We touchdown smoothly and roll along between the twin blur of edge lights, gradually slowing as thrust reversers and brakes catch us. When we exit onto a dim line of green taxiway lights, Cary needs to stop the aircraft for a few seconds. We are facing directly into the lights of the famous gambling strip, miles away. Still, it is so bright it is ruining our night vision and we can't see outside well enough. We pull our sun visors down and peer beneath them, chuckling. Canadian pop crooner

Corey Hart's song, "Sunglasses at Night," morphs into my head-music soundtrack: "We use our sun visors at night." We park at our gate on time. Our sleepy passengers instantly revive with anticipation and leave the plane smiling and fully energized. Meanwhile, we face a three-hour wait, then we'll do it all again, going home.

18

LAS2 Keep on Trucking

✈ ✈ ✈

First Officer's Log:
November 1984 / DC-9 /
LAS (Las Vegas) to YWG (Winnipeg)

The easy part of our day's work—or rather, *night's* work—is over. Now we face our next challenge—killing this three-hour stopover, then staying awake for the homeward leg.

This is our first trip in our month's work. We have several more to look forward to. As the month progresses, we will hear of other crews passing this time by taking a cab downtown to play tourist for an hour or so. Tonight, I prefer to sleep. I rummage around in the overhead bins to find some blankets and a pillow and wander further into the dim cabin, walking quietly so as not to disturb the flight attendants who have the same idea.

I find an aisle near the back row, flip up the armrests and with a little creative folding and bending, I manage to install my six-foot-two-inch frame into the four-foot-long seat rack. I place my hips and ribs in the least uncomfortable lumps, bumps and ridges, prop my neck up against the outboard wall with the tiny airline pillow wedged into the crick of my neck and set myself to fall asleep, hoping to not wake up later with my neck permanently bent at a forty-five-degree angle.

Surprisingly, I actually fall asleep. I'm jolted awake by the thumps of the front galley door swinging open and latching against the outer hull, followed by the metallic crash of a steel plank dropping into place, creating a bridge to the food service truck. The sounds of galley carts being wheeled in and slammed into their cabinets, accompanied by the raucous shouts of the galley service crew, forces me fully awake. Departure time must be near.

I slowly unmake my nest, put myself back together and shuffle outside into fresh night air, down to the ramp to find our office and pick up the printed copy of our flight plan. Cary is already there, looking about as sleepy as I feel. The weather going home is unchanged. Everything looks routine. We head upstairs and pick our way through the stream of passengers now wending their way on board. Most are looking pretty glum, worn out, sleepy and a little worse for wear after their "lost weekend" in Lost Wages. "So!" I nod and say cheerfully to the few people who are awake enough to make eye contact, "How much did you win? Anyone hit the jackpot?" I see a few tired grins and chuckles and one fellow pulls out the bottoms of his jacket pockets—the iconic *totally broke* gesture.

Cary and I get quickly to work, slurping the hot coffee our flight attendant reaches in to us. It's my leg home so I begin the ramp check procedures while Cary gathers up the needed information and clearances on the radio. The push-back and departure are routine and we blast off once more into the lonely night, or rather morning, eastbound. I'm thankful it's not summer because then we'd soon be facing the early sunrise. Nothing feels worse than sleep-deprived eyeballs squinting against a blaring sun. So, I relish the darkness and hope it lasts all the way home. My strategy for overnighters in the depths of winter is to fool myself into thinking I'm just finishing a long night's work. To this end, I dislike it if near the end of the flight, the controllers start wishing us a "good morning" when we check in on the radio. The longer I can fool my brain into thinking it's still last night, the better chance I have of sleeping once I get home.

These irregular schedules represent some of the best and worst of my working conditions. Pilots are away from home for long periods of time, but then we're home for longer periods as well. I enjoy being home and being involved in my kids' lives. I like greeting them at lunch and being there after school. But then, I am also away a lot and miss many of their special events. Successful airline families learn to creatively adjust. They make their own special times and celebrate Christmases and Birthdays on whichever day works out.

The erratic working hours also mean that I see a lot of spectacular sunrises and sunsets from my unique vantage point above the clouds. When Haley's comet was transiting our solar system, I happened to fly several late flights from Montreal to west coast cities. Many nights I had the best seat in the house, high over the mid-continent with a front row view of this brilliant comet. I tracked its progress as the tail flared off at progressive angles each trip and the comet passed before a changing backdrop of constellations. I, like Captain Cary on this night, moved my chair up close to the window in the darkened flight deck. There I sat in silence, wondering.

As these Las Vegas overnighters unfolded, my strategies for staying awake evolved. I discovered that snacking on unshelled sunflower seeds helped keep me alert. I don't know why, but it sure helped. Then there was the challenge of keeping both pilots happy with the temperature in the flight deck. I wanted to be warm and cozy especially on my feet, with a nice cool jet of air on my face. Cary liked things much the same so we got along. But sometimes, like old married couples, crew members have been known to get a little pouty about not being able to have the flight deck temperature exactly where they like it.

On long flights, the corners, nooks and outer walls of our tiny cabin get chilly due to the cold soak on the outside of the plane. I've never calculated the wind-chill factor for minus 50 with a 500 mph wind but after a few hours, the cold penetrates and radiates from the walls and floor. Keeping two pilots comfortable on the DC-9 was easy compared to my days as second officer on the B727. That cockpit was longer and relatively narrower. The two front pilots each froze their outboard arms, while the second officer sat cozily in the rear seat in the middle. They'd keep asking us to turn up the heat and the only way to satisfy them was for us to sit sweltering in a flight deck sauna. We second officers used to joke about buying a sweater, cutting it in half and lending each piece to our captains and first officers.

Interesting conversations also help pass the night when the airwaves are quiet and the whole earth seems still. Cary and I hit it off that way, often finding interesting topics to chat about. Over the month I heard stories of his younger days dabbling in commodity trading. "The guy at the ticker tape reader ahead of me suddenly turned pale, stumbled back into a chair and just kept saying, 'I'm ruined, I'm ruined...'" Note to self: never dabble in commodities.

Other times we'd chat about the successful business he owned. More than one airline pilot runs a business on the side. I think it's because many pilots are over-achievers and goal-oriented people. They need an ongoing challenge. Once the routine aspects of flying are mastered, they are driven to strike out further, looking for new challenges. Also, it's a way to counter the ever-present insecurity of this career.

I recall McPlane's presentation, back in the new-hire course, how only one in three pilots make it to full retirement age. Besides the many times when we are tested to renew our licenses, even minor medical issues can arise that wouldn't affect people in other jobs but will ground pilots, destroying our livelihoods.

Cary owned a plastics production plant. A few months after these Las Vegas charters, we were paired up again for a series of weekly trips to Alberta. Cary packed along a couple of four-foot-long white and black striped plastic tubes which he secured in the back of the flight deck. "I'm bidding on a contract to replace the wooden highway marker posts," he said. He had an appointment the next morning with the provincial highways department to deliver these prototypes so they could test them to see how they hold up through a prairie winter. That wasn't the strangest thing I've known pilots to transport. A friend, while working as second officer on the Lockheed L1011, once carried home a complete automobile fender he purchased while laying over in Los Angeles. It was for an antique car he was restoring. The Lockheed had a large flight deck closet where it fit nicely.

We also routinely, and in a more official capacity, transported live organs on the flight deck. An ambulance driver would hand us a picnic cooler at departure time and another would meet us to pick it up at our flight deck door on arrival. I used to look at these innocuous, red and white coolers—the same kind you can buy at any camping supply store—and wondered what weighty issues of life and death they represented. I thought about the two strangers who we would never meet, but whose lives were linked by this mundane plastic container. One lying in either a morgue or a recovery room, depending on the specific organ involved, the other now being prepped for surgery at our destination. Call it my dark sense of humor, but this little cooler spoke loudly to me of our responsibility to do our jobs carefully. We had no desire to create any more organ donors or recipients.

The hours homebound, especially between 2–4 am, were the hardest to get through. The airwaves were quiet. We would occasionally hear another night flight checking in or leaving the ATC frequency. I wondered who or what they might be transporting. Often they were freighter pilots, frequent denizens of the night skies, especially with the growing success of FedEx and their competitors. If we happened to pass within sight of one another we'd exchange a greeting by turning on some outside lights, and then try to spot them before they reported seeing us.

As the month progressed I resorted to other creative tactics to stay alert in flight. When driving long highway trips, I enjoy listening to music. The latest, state-of-the-art portable music devices of the day, the Sony Walkman, were definitely against the rules for flight deck use. But I figured it was fair game if I used one of our built-in navigation radios, the *ADF (Automatic Direction Finder)* to listen to the airwaves. ADF radios are normally used to point towards specific navigation stations. But they can also tune the frequencies used by commercial AM radio broadcasters. By keeping the volume low in my headset, I could listen in without missing the infrequent ATC calls on the main radio. I would idly scan the public broadcast bands. It's surprising how far radio waves travel in the night sky. Certain stations in North America are allowed to boost their signal strength at night, extending their range. I could find channels from Alaska to Newfoundland and all the way to Florida. The quality shifted unsteadily as we moved through the atmosphere at eight miles a minute, so I'd frequently abandon one station to search for another. It kept my mind active.

About halfway through the month, I discovered a super-station broadcasting from Lincoln, Nebraska. They specialized in playing requests for the night-time truckers moving the nation's goods along lonely highways. Few if any big rigs of the time had phones in their cabs, but the drivers would call from favorite roadside stops to ask for a song, chat a little and report the weather and road conditions. The DJ would put these calls on the air. As I listened in, I came to identify with these fellow night drivers. Though they were hauling goods and we were hauling spent gamblers, and although their big rigs might have 18 wheels while ours only had six, still I felt like we were kindred spirits.

As the month progressed I came to recognize some of the regular callers. For example, Big Mike drove up and down the west coast. "Yeah, the I-5 is in good shape tonight, 'cept for some fog in the valleys just south of Seattle...." Or, "Road Bear calling, just to say there are a few rain showers in northern Florida, and to request my favorite song. I'd like to dedicate this to the wife and kids." There would be more technical reports as well, as the DJ queried the callers about their rigs and trips: "I'm driving a Kenworth from Vancouver to Phoenix. I wonder if you have any road reports from other drivers along the route...."

In a way, I guess this was a glimpse of how social media was to develop over the next few decades. I began to imagine how it would sound if I called in. "Howdy! This is Sky Driver, calling in. I'm just about six miles out of Casper, Wyoming (as in six miles high!). Weather's looking nice and clear here, all the way along to the Canadian border. I'm wheeling just six big donuts but we're good and heavy tonight at 98,000 pounds ... I'd like to request ..." I never got up my nerve to make the call, but I'm sure a lot of listeners might have enjoyed the humor as they figured out what kind of rig I was "driving."

Finally, on descent, about 120 miles outside of Winnipeg, I'd lose the last of the truck station signals. It was time to get ready for landing and soon we'd be drifting earthward once more, leaving the sky to the daytime pilots who would soon be taking off with the sun, as it pushed its way above the eastern horizon.

The November nights flew by, and soon I was back on a more normal work cycle. Though it was challenging for a day-hawk like myself to work so many all-nighters, it was a great way to get to know "Smokey" a lot better. We flew many more trips together over the years, but November's trial-by-sleep-deprivation was unique. I wonder if that AM radio station is still out there broadcasting, keeping lonely night-truckers and all-night-flyers awake and safe on the night highways and skyways.

19

CARBON VS. SILICON

✈   ✈   ✈

The real danger is not that computers will begin to think like men,
but that men will begin to think like computers. – Sydney J. Harris

Humans are the only creatures in the world that possess the powers
of complex creativity. We have a unique ability to draw ideas from the
surrounding ether and invent such beautiful things as songs, stories,
poems, paintings and technological wonders of every description. Our
creativity is a mystery. Even the great artists admit it. Leonard Cohen
once said, "If I knew where the good songs come from I'd go there
more often."

Creativity seems to be related to free will. How we use our creative
powers determines the kind of world we live in. We have used our creative free will to develop rules that help us function in complex social
structures. The development of a rule-based society—the so-called
"rule of law"—is a hallmark of our civilization. Sometimes tension
arises between our free will and our need to follow rules, especially if
the rules are wrong, outdated or immoral. To remain valid, rules must
be constantly reviewed and tweaked or totally rewritten. That is the
responsibility of we-the-humans. Carbon is the key element in our human physiology so I sometimes allude to this power of free will and
creativity within us by calling humans ***carbon-based units.***

How do we carbon-based units adapt to the inherent inadequacies
of rules? The key is for us to discern the intent of the rule. The spirit of
the rule. Knowing what is behind the rules provides us with the wisdom
we need to know when and how and to what degree we should be following the rules. If we are compassionate, caring beings who consider
the needs of those around us to be as significant as our own, our rulebook can be very slim. The rulebook becomes thicker as we try to in-
hibit the damage caused by selfishness and other anti-social behavior.

Blatantly ignoring rules creates dangers as well. It is the breakdown
of civilization. In a human body, cells that go rogue and completely

ignore the rules to which they are designed are called cancers.

Humans invented computers that illustrate the ultimate in rule-following. By definition, that's what they are, that's what they do. They follow a prescribed list of instructions. Consequently, computers have no moral struggles. They do not worry about the choices they make. Nor do they lie awake at night worrying about the choices they'll make tomorrow. Terms like *worry* and *think* and other anthropomorphisms are misleading. We use them too easily when referring to computers and almost forget that computers are not conscious beings. They have no willpower. They have no free will. If a computer were considered human, it would need to be locked up as a menace to society.

By any human description of personality, computers are obsessive-compulsive, dispassionate psychopaths. Computers process a list of rules, period. That's all they do. That's all they can do. And herein lies their inescapable limitation. *Rules contain an inherent weakness.* They can never completely describe the continually-changing, dynamic and downright chaotic universe we occupy.

Silicon is the key ingredient in our computers, so I describe rule-based behavior by that term. Computers are ***silicon-based units***. Silicon-based units are great tools but they are never great masters. Carbon must always remain in control of silicon. We created silicon-based, computer-driven devices to serve us. We do not serve them. Likewise, if we forget that rules are meant to serve our needs rather than the other way around, we create a disaster. If we limit ourselves to rules and *think* like computers, we diminish ourselves. We fall short of our potential.

20

Fog Bound – Carbon vs. Silicon 2

✈   ✈   ✈

First Officer's Log:
1980 / DC-9 / Morning Departure
YYC (Calgary) to YQR (Regina)

"Visibility is below limits," I tell Captain Dent as I click off the recorded *ATIS (Automatic Terminal Information Service)* message in my headset. I've scrawled the pertinent information on a chit of paper which I drop onto the center console. He leans in to read it. Dent looks at me strangely because outside our cockpit windows, the sun is blazing above the morning horizon. We see nothing but blue skies and unlimited visibility in all directions—*CAVU (Ceiling and Visibility Unlimited)* in pilot talk. The devices measuring visibility sit on the grass beside the touchdown zone of the active runway, at the south end of the airport. We're parked at the terminal building two miles away. That runway zone is notorious for strange readings because it is located in a shallow depression which often fills with fog. Like this morning.

Over the years, and especially since becoming a pilot, I have learned how we humans wrestle with our rules. Rules are never perfect. They can never keep up with the changing chaos of reality. Rules are rules, so we have to follow them—but judiciously. This is something we learn by experience and today looks like a learning opportunity.

A recent amendment to our regulations gives the readings from silicon-based, chip-driven sensors top priority. Time was, qualified carbon-based human beings could overrule the electronic readouts. Not today. In one stroke of the pen, pilots and air-traffic controllers have been declared untrustworthy to gauge distance by known references—something we have been doing successfully until now.

Dent picks up his mic, punches the transmit button and calls the control tower. From their vantage point high above the airport, they confirm there is a fog patch over the first 2000 feet of runway 34. The remaining 10,000 feet is in the clear. The secondary runway is closed all day for maintenance.

Regulations are in flux. New technology is coming into use allowing pilots to operate safely in poor visibility. Airlines have invested millions of dollars in new aircraft equipment and pilot training. The payoff is supposed to be better on-time performance despite bad weather. Nobody likes to see flights delayed or cancelled. The airports are doing their part by upgrading runways as well. Consequently, rule-makers are scrambling to keep up, but sometimes, when they adjust regulations to accommodate new capabilities, they create unintended consequences. Like now. Reality versus rules. This is always a struggle. Today Captain Dent intends to strike a blow for carbon-based units and common sense.

"Let's plan for an **intersection departure** and we'll stay clear of the fog," Dent says to me. "I'll fill out the incident form later to cover my backside. Don't let me forget." Dent knows the DC-9 well. We have charts assuring us that there is more than adequate fog-free runway for a safe takeoff. This procedure is called an *intersection takeoff* and it is a standard procedure but one we don't often use. We will start our roll from a little further along the runway at another access point. All the safety requirements will be met or surpassed. The only fly in the ointment is that the tower log may show that we departed when the official visibility was below limits. By filling out an incident report, Dent is keeping our Chief Pilot in the loop. He is known to be a fair and practical man, and Dent is confident of his support. However, no Chief Pilot likes to receive a surprise call from Transport Canada about operational irregularities. If anyone questions Dent's decision, our Chief Pilot will be forewarned.

Dent and I calculate our takeoff settings, push back, start the engines and begin our two-mile taxi. It's a wonderful spring morning and I enjoy watching our shadow tracking beside us as we make our way southbound. We are on a taxiway that parallels the main runway, which means we get a good chance to view the entire airport. As reported, there are no fog patches anywhere but at the button of the runway. I'm monitoring the company radio, waiting for our final load information. When we have "the numbers," that is, the details of our weight and balance, I will confirm everything is correct, we'll finish our checklist and go. That's when I hear another captain still parked at the gate, cancel his flight. "The visibility is below requirements." I look at Captain Dent and he shrugs. Different strokes for different folks. While Dent, with my concurrence, is choosing the operational "what's safe and makes sense" *modus operandi*, it seems our colleagues have chosen to abide strictly by the rules, verbatim. I don't like such literal interpretation of rules. It offends my sense of common sense, not to mention economic sense. Canceling a flight is a big-ticket item. Local staff will be scrambling to deal with the sudden changes—not to mention customer ill will.

On the other hand, such costly cancellations will motivate management to get this broken situation fixed as soon as possible. But for now, the silicon-based readouts, empowered by poorly-written regulations, have inconvenienced travelers, costing our airline cash and goodwill. All this while providing zero benefits for safety. This is not the intent of the rule. But that flight is canceled and the damage is done. In this game of rules versus reality, the score becomes: Silicon: one. Carbon: zero.

But hang on. We two carbon-based units are moving into scoring position. Dent decides to taxi all the way to the beginning of the runway to assess the fog up close. He follows the yellow line into the haze and as we move northward on the runway centerline we soon have enough visibility to satisfy the requirements. He pours on full power and we accelerate rapidly out of the last of the fog into the bright sun and away we go. Score tied. Silicon: one. Carbon: one.

As we climb into the morning skies of Calgary, we arc eastwards to Regina, turning our backs on the sunlit Rockies. We fumble our translucent visors down to reduce the squint factor from the sun still low on the horizon ahead. In our headsets, we hear other flights working Calgary ATC. A corporate jet executes a missed approach. He wants to land from the other end of the runway. The prevailing wind is light and this is an entirely logical idea. Score one more point for carbon. Silicon: one; Carbon: two.

But silicon thinking isn't easily vanquished. The air traffic controller tells Bizjet Pilot there will be a long delay. There are several more airplanes on final. *Oh, great,* I think to myself with a mental face-palm.

More flights that can't land. The entire conga line could be re-routed to approach from the opposite direction and never go near the fog. Low lying fog can be a strange phenomenon. As pilots fly down the electronic glide slope, we can see the runway through the mist well enough to continue, fully expecting to land. Then as we descend into the fog, our visibility can suddenly drop to near zero. Finding the runway by Braille is not considered an acceptable technique. So, a surprised pilot is forced to add power and pull back into the sky in what is called a *"go-around"* or a "balked landing" or a "missed approach."

Whichever term you use, they all represent delays and increased costs to the airlines. This morning, the air traffic controllers show no intention of changing the active runway. I cynically imagine they are laying bets to see which flights land and which ones go around. Illogically, the flights are kept approaching into the fog. Silicon thinking fights back to tie the score. Silicon: two. Carbon: two.

We do a quick turn-around at Regina and while the morning is still young, we're on our way back to Calgary. I'm expecting to see either the fog has burned off or the other runway in use. But no. Flights are still trying to touch down in minimal visibility. The isolated fog bank still covers the touchdown zone. Silicon "thinking" seems determined to win today's contest. I reluctantly award another point for this lack of initiative. Silicon: 3. Carbon: 2.

Can we come from behind at the last minute? Dent, in accordance with our SOPs, has given me this leg to fly back to Calgary. We talk things over. We would like to avoid the fog and find a more carbon-friendly approach. We could request to land on the opposite end of the strip, but that would incur a delay as happened to the BizJet earlier. We decide to stay above the electronic glide slope and land by visual means on the pavement beyond. The remaining distance is still twice as much as we need.

Visual approaches are a basic piloting skill. It's how all pilots first learned to land. DC-9 pilots fly visual approaches regularly because we often land at small-town airports where the electronic aids are scarce or non-existent. Despite the growing perception that airliners are flown by computers chasing electronic signals, this is simply not true, especially of our older-generation DC-9. Once again, we intend to prove that carbon rules. We cross the ***final approach fix,*** which is four miles from the runway, at a thousand feet above the ground. I set up a smooth descent keeping us above the fog. We touch down gently with no surprises and turn off the runway with a mile left over. Score tied again: three all!

Our score for this day ended in a tie. I'm not sure how anyone else's scores turned out. For our next departure two hours later, the fog had lifted and operations were back to normal. I continue wondering about humans and our uneasy relationship with rules and bureaucracy and limited silicon logic. At least this one morning we battled valiantly for free carbon! *Vive le Carbon Libre!*

Afterthoughts

I am not advocating that anyone, least of all pilots, blatantly disregard rules. There's a quote attributed to G.K. Chesterton that says: "Before removing a fence, always pause to ask why it was placed there in the first place..." Living by the rules requires thought and judgment. This seems ironic, doesn't it? We sometimes want rules to absolve us of responsibility, thinking we need only practice obedience. But that philosophy has historically caused terrible disasters. Blind obedience to rules is never good enough because rules can never adequately handle the relentless chaos of reality.

Soon after the events described in this story, the Canadian ATC system transformed into a crown corporation called NavCanada and things began to improve. The old bureaucratic attitude used to be: "Airplanes aren't colliding so I am doing my job." Under NavCanada, a new service-oriented attitude emerged that seemed to say: "How can we help our customers, the pilots and their passengers safely and efficiently reach their destinations?" This new philosophy was a breath of fresh air. Well-trained, well-motivated humans prove time and again that the creative, responsible thinking of carbon-based units, rules.

As it should.

Note: *Regulations were eventually modified to account for the complications caused by localized phenomena.*

21

Captain N.D. Cision

✈   ✈   ✈

The captain may not always be right, but he's always the captain.
The first officer's *duty is to assist and support the captain—except*
when it's not.

First Officer's Log:
1984 / DC-9 / Departing YUL (Montreal)

For the third time, the captain reaches tentatively to the overhead
panel as if to turn off the seatbelt switch, then hesitates and withdraws
his hand. I've never flown with Captain N.D. Cision before. He's new
on our base and all I know about him is he has recently been promoted
to captain and he was a first officer on the 747. Because of the way the
seniority system works, this implies that he has been a first officer for
an unusually long time.

We're on the early climb-out from Montreal and we've been experiencing pockets of light chop. We know the flight attendants are eager
to start the cabin service for this short hop to Toronto. At last the air
smooths out for several seconds and Captain N.D. switches off the
sign. But a few minutes later it's rough again. I see he is debating and
second-guessing whether he should put the sign back on. Then there is
a sharp knock at the cockpit door followed by the purser poking his
head in to say, "It's getting too rough back here, captain. We're going
to sit down again for a while. Can we get the seatbelt sign on again to
keep the passengers seated?" The captain complies.

As the day progresses, the captain seems continually reluctant to
make decisions. Airline pilots make a thousand decisions a day. Starting
in the flight planning phase and continuing until the final shutdown,
each flight comprises a never-ending flow of decisions. Some are
trivial. Many are crucial. Some must never be wrong.

We continually take stock of fuel loads, weather conditions and altitudes as we analyze flight plans and decide to stay the course or alter

them. We make choices about runways, flap configurations and a host of risks on every flight. The demands of safety are often at odds with short-term efficiency and we continually arbitrate. We make decisions about technical equipment malfunctions and evaluate the inherent risks of flying with missing equipment or insisting it be fixed. Just because something is legal doesn't mean it's safe enough. We are constantly gathering information to develop our situational awareness. From this, we project into the future as best we can to avoid unpleasant surprises. An old aviation adage says: *Never let your airplane go anywhere your mind hasn't already been.*

Flight after flight, I grow more uneasy with Captain N.D.'s discomfort calling the shots. I'm not enjoying this. The roles of captain and first officer are clearly delineated. He has the authority. Even when he delegates decisions to me, it must be clear that I am operating in his name—by his authority. If the tail starts wagging the dog, bad things can happen.

Two days later we're on the second to last flight of our three days together. We're en route from **YHZ** (Halifax) to **BOS** (Boston). The weather along the route is good. But as we near Boston we see an unexpected line of thunderstorms on the horizon. They are drifting across Boston from the northwest towards the east into the Atlantic Ocean.

Flying near thunderstorms is one of the most demanding things pilots do. These intense packets of energy pose several threats. Hail is the worst. Smashing into solid ice at the speeds we fly can destroy an aircraft's wings, engines and windshield in short order. More common are hazards from turbulence and **wind-shear**, especially near the ground. Downbursts can tumble and shift and swirl violently, testing the controllability of any airliner. Intense rain obscures the pilot's view while rain-drenched runways pose braking and steering problems. Lightning is impressive but only poses a minor risk to the airplane's structure, because fuselages are bonded and equipped with static discharge wicks. Still, a sudden flash can temporarily blind the pilots, especially at night.

Furthermore, thunderstorms are dynamic. They form, move, then dissipate quickly and sometimes with very little warning. When we have open space to maneuver we can stay clear of the hazards—provided we have adequate fuel. But when storms are sweeping across one of the busiest airports in the country, the airspace suddenly gets congested. Too many aircraft all need to occupy a reduced set of storm-free, space-time coordinates.

The pressure on the people working in this environment grows exponentially. Everyone simultaneously needs to arrange detours around the storm cells. The frequencies are congested, making communication difficult at a time when clear communications are critical. On days like this, I am frustrated that we are stuck using slightly updated versions of an old system that was already in use back in the era of DC3s. Our so-called two-way radios only allow one person to speak at a time. No one knows if someone else is about to speak. The piercing electronic squeal caused when two people push their transmit buttons at the same time grates on the nerves and adds to the confusion.

As we start our descent towards Logan, I'm double-checking our fuel load. We have enough to fly back to Yarmouth on the near coast of Nova Scotia. I pull up the latest weather reports on our data-link to make sure Yarmouth is still solid—it is. We are also carrying a few extra pounds of kerosene because this is **BOS** at a busy time of the day. We routinely carry extra to account for heavy traffic flow or unplanned holds. We'll have about 30 minutes of "happy gas" in reserve. It should be enough. But in these conditions, more would be even better.

It's becoming clear we are going to arrive at the same time as the storms. I wonder aloud if Captain N.D. would like to maneuver to the backside of this line while we are still high up and can pick our way westward through "the tops." I've seen this strategy work before. I try to drop a hint. "What do you think about trying to get onto the west side of this line right now and descending behind the storms?" Okay, it's a pretty strong hint. No response, although I'm sure he heard me.

As we continue our descent along our route this option is taken away. We are now committed to descending on the eastern side. Maybe he's hoping to beat the squall line to the airport. But it's not working out. More likely, I fear he's hoping ATC will lead us into a gap in the storms closer to the field and relieve him from having to make the decision.

Below us, we can see flights departing and heading east over the water. This at least tells us that flights are finding the storms navigable. They must be finding holes between the worst of the rain shafts down low. They are picking their way through using the ***Mark One Human***

Eyeball combined with their weather radar.

Weather radar has limitations, especially when we're down low in close to the rain shafts. The antennae can only pitch upwards a few degrees. I've seen experienced captains with good instincts and sharp eyes find the best pathway through a line by staying relatively low, below the bases of the clouds, where they could see and avoid the heaviest rain shafts. In truth, sometimes finding a path through storms involves as much art and luck as it does science.

Soon we are below ten thousand feet and ATC tries to give us a heading to our right, towards the west, to get us to the western side of the airport. This would line us up with the approach path and fit us into the flow of traffic. The controller knows about the storms but her radar is not specialized for detecting weather—only airplanes. She offers us a route in trail of other flights which are reportedly getting through with only moderate turbulence. I'm busy twiddling the radar antenna to pull the best picture from the storm cells. I see a couple of potential spots in the direction she wants us to head where we could get through. I point them out to Captain N.D. but the associated clouds look dark and ominous. This effect is magnified by the angle of the sun. He refuses to accept the heading she offers. "Unable," he says.

I'm pretty sure we'd be safe to turn westerly at several spots. Other flights have recently gone through. There are no reports of hail. Probably the worst thing we'd face would be a few minutes of heavy rain, and some memorable bumps. The captain tentatively starts a turn toward one such hole on the radar picture but then turns back. We're now down to 5,000 feet and still heading southbound. We'll soon be cutting through Boston's departure paths. I can hear the tension in the controller's voice as she asks us if it looks good for turning westerly yet. The captain shakes his head and says, "No, I want to stay on this heading. Maybe there's a way to get around the south end..."

The controller rapidly assigns us to a new frequency. We now switch to the departure controller who is working the sector of departing flights fanning out ahead of us. As I tune the frequency, I immediately hear him assigning lower altitudes to the aircraft climbing eastbound. "Eastern 123, altitude now amended to 3,000. Do not climb above 3,000." Eastern responds. I can only imagine how much this controller doesn't want us cutting across his departure paths. I finally get a chance to jump into the mix and report on the frequency. "Radar identified. Take up a turn to the west as soon as you can, please."

But there is nothing Captain N.D. likes well enough to stick his nose in. He refuses to bite the bullet, to pull our seatbelts up tight and head between the cells as best we can. The storms are drifting eastward pushing us further offshore, further away from the runways. I'm watching our fuel level. I've already calculated a "Bingo" fuel quantity to get us safely back to Yarmouth. But it's hard to know how much to adjust for the fact that we're still heading south and getting further and further away.

We're now south of the departure paths but we still see a long line of storms ahead, stretching for miles. N.D.'s hope of finding a way around the southern end is not going to work. He says "get me a 180-degree turn. We'll have to keep looking back to the north." I reluctantly key the microphone, imagining the inner groan from the controller who clears us to make the turn. We will be plowing back across the departure paths again. He was busy enough without the extra complication. He's about to get even busier. The turn takes us further from Boston, toward the east and through to the north. At least now Captain N.D. has the storms on his side of the plane. Maybe this will help him find an acceptable hole.

So we begin our way north again, pushed further and further from the airport by the offshore drift of the squalls. We are about 20 miles east of the airport now and if we don't turn inbound soon, things are going to get very tense fuel-wise. I'm busy communicating with ATC as we change frequencies again. I listen for an opening in the constant chatter to check in without talking over some else. I'm also tweaking the radar antenna, looking for clear spots while recalculating our fuel in my head. We are approaching minimum fuel for diverting to Yarmouth. I tell the captain this in a loud, clear voice to ensure he hears me over the noises in his headset. No response. I'm feeling isolated as I glance down at the cold whitecaps streaming off the waves below and up at the storms still towering above us and cutting us off from the airport. I didn't bring my bathing suit.

We drone northward through the departure tracks again, with more frequency changes and hurried re-clearances by controllers to keep other flights below us or send them tracking around us. It doesn't take much imagination to know how unpopular we are in Boston's radar room right now. The tension in the controller's voices says it all.

My own tension is rising as well. Our fuel situation is approaching a critical point. The captain still hasn't found any holes in the clouds suiting his exacting standards. I see him glancing back over his shoulder along the line of weather as if he's contemplating another turn back towards the south. I pick a spot on our track ahead and set a *"No Go"* point in my mind. At that place, just two minutes ahead, either we will be turned towards Boston's Logan airport, or we must be diverting towards Yarmouth. At that point, we will have only the minimum fuel legally required to reach our alternate.

What we cannot do—must not do—is turn south again. Along that path, we lose all landing options besides Boston. Along that course, we lose our choices about where to penetrate the storms. If we pick the wrong spot, the outcome could be a disaster. If we delay too long, a southward path presents a real danger of running out of fuel.

I'm hoping Captain N.D. isn't seriously planning to turn south again. I'm hoping I won't have to mutiny and fight for the controls. But I'm silently rehearsing how I will form my demand that we divert to Yarmouth. I realize I must be prepared to mutiny to ensure the safety of the flight. They never trained us for this in flight school.

We're getting close to the line in the sky I've drawn. I feel my pulse, which has been on overdrive for too long already, thumping ever louder. I wonder briefly if a sudden aneurysm on my part will cause N.D. to divert to our alternate. Then he spots a Northwest B727 below and slightly ahead of us on his side of the plane. Simultaneously, I hear the Northwest Airlines pilot on the frequency saying, "Yeah, I think we'll be able to turn in towards the airport right about here..." By craning my neck, I see the silhouetted Boeing curving towards the west. Captain N.D. quickly says, "We'll follow him. Tell ATC we're turning in behind him."

No one is more relieved by this decision than me. But the controller's voice also reveals a tone of thankfulness. I am saved from forcing the issue—mutiny avoided. No need to flee to a tropical island where I can hide from justice, like the first mate in *Mutiny on the Bounty*. Besides, I don't think there are any palm trees in Nova Scotia anyway.

We plunge through the clouds and rain with some moderate rattling and rolling. The controller assigns us headings to mimic the path of the Northwest 727. She asks for a slower speed to create the needed space to begin clearing us down to lower altitudes behind the Boeing. The rest of the flight is routine. We make a sweeping turn out towards the west of Boston, from where we catch the approach to the eastbound runway. We're in the bright sunlight for most of it; the storms continue receding to the east. The airport is again running at a normal pace, and only the rain-soaked asphalt attests to the fact that there was any weather here at all.

After a quick "we're running late" stop, refuel and reload, we're on our way to Montreal for the last leg of the three-day trip. The weather is clear and smooth, but my mind is a turmoil. I've never before flown with a captain who dislikes making decisions. I struggle, wondering what to do. Captain N.D. Cision's performance is not up to standards, at least in my opinion. I'd never been in such an uncomfortable spot since becoming a pilot. If I share my misgivings to company or union officials, I am undermining a colleague's livelihood and professional standing. If I say nothing, I am ignoring my larger responsibilities to my company, my profession and ultimately to our passengers.

It is late when we get home and whatever I decide to do has to wait until morning when offices reopen. I pass a sleepless night. Early next morning before I have time to act, a union representative calls me. There have been other first officers raising concerns. He asks what my experience of N.D. was like. I tell him. As far as I know, N.D. never again flew as captain.

22

Blippity Blip Blip, Doctors

✈   ✈   ✈

Doctors are men who prescribe medicines of which they know little, to cure diseases of which they know less, in human beings of whom they know nothing. –attributed to Voltaire (1694-1778)

I'm lying on the exam table like Dr. Frankenstein's monster, with wires running from my ankles, arms and chest to an EKG machine. It's a pilot's least favorite event—the annual medical checkup. I've been through this so many times I know it all by heart. And it's my heart I'm fixating on as I try to calm the blippity-blip-blips of my pulse. The EKG machine emits a few seconds of whirring, followed by a few more tense seconds of silence while it ruminates. Then the machine spits out a long strip of paper. All routine. But suddenly not. The nurse frowns at the printout, excuses herself, then hurries out of the room. That's never happened before. Now my pulse is really racing.

She returns with Dr. Clouseau. That's the nickname assigned to him by *line pilots*. It is fully intended to bring up images of the hapless inspector, made famous in movies by Peter Sellers. Clouseau studies the strip of paper with its mysterious wavy lines, frowns darkly and says, "Get dressed and come see me in my office." Then he turns and leaves. His usual abrupt manner makes me think he missed any lectures in Med School about treating human beings instead of diseases.

Fifty percent of doctors are below average. Or to be more accurate, below the median. No matter how I say it, I'm sure you get the message. Regardless of how they do in medical school, after graduation, a doctor's competence comes down to what he or she does to keep updating and improving their knowledge and skills. The same is true for everyone. When all is said and done, some doctors are going to occupy that lower half of the Bell Curve. This is definitely Dr. Clouseau's domain. Since he came on staff at our company clinic, pilots are having more frequent problems with mandatory medical checkups. We line pilots might be exaggerating when we claim that Dr. C's goal is to enhance air safety by disqualifying all pilots—but not by much.

Recurrent medical exams at six- or twelve-month intervals (depending on our age) represent one more hurdle airline pilots must leap— one more "opportunity" to lose our license and our livelihood. The longer I was in this profession with these constant, recurrent tests of fitness and ability, the more I resented doctors who judged my status without submitting to any ongoing checks of their own competence. Who is checking the checkers? We pilots can frequently be heard moaning about this state of affairs when we gather and commiserate with colleagues who are facing their ongoing *trials-by-medico*. We all have our stories. We are all understandably nervous of this power doctors hold over us. More than one pilot suffers from what is termed "white coat syndrome," where blood pressure escalates several points the moment a doctor enters the examining room. The old joke is often recycled amongst flyers: what's the difference between doctors and pilots? Doctors bury their mistakes. Pilots are buried *by* their mistakes.

Dr. Clouseau sits across his big desk, staring dourly at me as he says, "You have a new heartbeat irregularity. I can't sign your license." He pushes my pilot's license back across the glass desktop. The all-important line, needing his signature, remains blank. With that simple gesture, he has crashed my world. Later that day as I sit at home, head spinning, my phone rings and the chief of our medical clinic is calling. As far as Dr. Clouseau sits below the average, our head physician, Dr. Tee sits above it. He is an ex-Air Force medico, and unlike Clouseau, Dr. Tee actually likes airplanes, flying and pilots. He is a sharp cookie. He understands the aviation industry and the concept of appropriate risk management.

"Come into my office tomorrow on your way to work. I'll sign your license so you can go do your flight. I see no reason that you shouldn't keep flying while we research this new heartbeat." He goes on to explain that a small percentage of people develop this kind of heart tick. If there are no other complicating factors it is considered a normal abnormality. I feel the relief flow over me.

My relief turns out to be temporary. After a few weeks and a battery of tests, we discover I have inflammation in my lungs. A diagnosis of a rare, chronic inflammatory disease called *sarcoidosis* grounds me. And floors me. The gist of Dr. Tee's explanation goes like this: "Your immune system is attacking itself. We don't know why. We don't know for sure if that's also the cause of your heart irregularity. The symptoms usually resolve in time. If they don't, it's usually treatable."

But I'm an airline pilot and there is no track record that suggests how this will play out. Apparently, it's really embarrassing for the doctor who signed my license to have me die at the flight controls. There is no way to prove a connection between this autoimmune disorder and the heartbeat irregularity, aside from performing an autopsy—something I'm keen on avoiding. When I push further I get an opinion that as long as I don't drop dead, *after a certain length of time*, and if nothing else bad happens, *after a certain length of time*, then maybe eventually there's a chance, *after a certain length of time*, to get my license back—maybe. No one is willing to guess how long that "certain length of time" might be. So, what can I do? Basically, wait and see if I drop dead from heart failure. Sharing my own dark sense of humor, Dr. Tee goes on to explain, "It's a pleasant way to die. As your brain goes into hypoxia, you will experience euphoria. How's that for the good news?" I wonder about this as I drive home.

During the struggle to re-establish my pilot privileges, I will visit more doctors than any person should ever have to. I discover a wide-ranging competency among the specialists and clinicians I consult. Dr. Clouseau-clones are in abundance as they righteously express opinions about my health based on twenty-year-old information they culled from medical school and have never updated. That, and their own fears of flying. Initially, lung specialists at one of Montreal's premier university clinics will prescribe an ultra-high dose of prednisone. My lung indicators will clear up. Unhappily, the heartbeat irregularity will not. Even more unhappily, my family and I are not warned that a side-effect of high doses of prednisone includes outbursts of rage. The wounds from this oversight will mark our family for decades.

Fifty percent of all doctors are below average. But that also means that many doctors are highly-gifted, thoughtful and intelligent. They work as hard at developing their professional standards as I do my own. I vow to seek help from such individuals and stay as far away as possible from the Clouseau-clones. It will require Herculean efforts—

or should I say Asklepiosian efforts (Asklepius was the Greek god of medicine)—to overcome the bureaucracy of Transport Canada. For now, no one knows if I will fly again—if I will ever continue pursuing my dream to become an airline captain.

23

Landing on my Feet

✈   ✈   ✈

I'm back in the new-hire pilot training classroom and once again, Mr. McPlane is explaining to a new, eager class of recruits how only one in three pilots will reach full retirement age. This time, however, I'm standing at the front of the classroom as an instructor, a potential member of that "other two" early retirement club. I am medically grounded. But because I am feeling good and need something to do, I called up my Base Manager and asked if there are any jobs I could take on while I sort through this medical issue. I jumped at this opportunity to work at the pilots' training school. I'm an instructor again. Life has a funny way of leading me around in circles. Hopefully, the circles actually form an ascending spiral, progressing toward something. Each time around feels the same—but different.

There is a hiring surge in these latter years of the 1980s, so it's an interesting time to be instructing. The new-hire pilots are much more qualified than many of us were a decade ago. It comes down to supply and demand. For many years, the industry was stagnant, so the candidates have gained significant experience piloting turbo-prop aircraft in regional airlines, high-performance business jets or military aircraft. They may be new to our company, but they are experienced aviators. Another change since the days I was hired is the gender of the new candidates. Every class of twenty includes one or two female pilots. The flight deck is one of the last bastions of male exclusivity in the company, and the addition of aviatrixes to the mix is long overdue. I recall two excellent female flight instructors who helped me in the early stages of my career. They would have loved the same opportunities I had but were excluded because of their chromosomal status. Thankfully, as Bob Dylan wrote, "The times, they are a changin'."

When I was hired in 1975, female airline pilots were extremely rare. I only knew of one in the entire country. Most of us knew her name. Rosella flew F-28s for a regional airline in Manitoba. The situation in other western countries was the same. This was sadly ironic, considering the contribution women pilots made to the war effort in the years just prior to the rapid expansion of the airline industry. During the war, women were flying new aircraft to the front and returning the battered, shot-up aircraft to be repaired or recycled for scrap. When the war ended, these highly-qualified pilots were unceremoniously dismissed to civilian life, sometimes with little recognition for their achievements. No one seemed to consider that they should begin careers as commercial pilots. Today, women still comprise only about five percent of the airline pilot workforce.

As the year progresses, I am assigned more responsibility for coordinating the new-hire courses. As enjoyable as it is, I am aware that in this setting, my opportunities for advancement and a long-term career are limited. Here, I will always be a sort of wounded duck—a grounded pilot. So, one day during lunch break, I listened with interest as I sat with two fellow instructors. They were talking about another ex-colleague who, just prior to my arrival, quit and took a job with a local aircraft manufacturer. "He's developing the training programs for that new Regional Jet."

A Canadian builder of business jets had ventured into a risky project, producing a 50-seat jet airplane to compete on the short feeder routes. Until now, a variety of turbo-prop powered aircraft or the smallest airliners, such as DC-9s or B-737s, served these routes. The existing jetliners were unprofitable and the turbo-prop aircraft were unpopular with passengers. The usual comments claimed, "They are noisy, bumpy, and slow, compared to *real* (i.e. jet airliner) airplanes."

This point of view was not wrong. Turbo-prop aircraft are noisy, due to the vibrations from the large propellers; bumpy, because they fly at lower altitudes where they encounter more turbulence from storm clouds; and slow, because the cruise speeds of most propeller-driven aircraft are almost 100 miles-per-hour less than jet-engined aircraft.

A smaller jet transport that could compete economically with turbo-props on short routes made a lot of sense. I immediately saw an enterprise with a great future. As for my own future, instructing in my current role was limiting. I tried to keep a positive outlook, but I was uncertain that I'd ever be allowed to resume my career in the flight deck. I had no idea if my dreams would ever get back on the rails. When these two colleagues suggested I call their buddy to ask about opportunities to help develop the pilot training for a new type of aircraft, I acted the same day. As so often happens in life, new opportunities come unexpectedly, often by word of mouth from friends and colleagues—networking.

Faster than expected, I'm hired. The next two years become a swirl of activity. We are literally inventing a new class of regional jet. A large Canadian transportation company—a company that started out building snowmobiles in the hinterlands of Quebec—is expanding to become an even larger player in the global transportation industry. They already produce world-class trains and business jets, and I am confident their new airliner will be successful as well. I am suddenly on the threshold of a new career path with exciting possibilities ahead.

In a turn of events I never could have foreseen, from the depths of disappointment, depression and confusion of being officially grounded, I'm now involved in the ground-floor development of an exciting new project. I am helping develop plans for facilities, computer-based training systems, latest-technology flight simulators and visual systems. I'm helping search for new personnel to fill key roles as we ramp up for ground-school and flight-simulator training. Our small cadre of people is constantly growing as we work furiously towards a target sales date, and as fast as we run, we can never catch up. It is exhilarating and exhausting. Within two years, we grow from three to twenty-five employees, and we're still hiring. All this before the airplane is even ready for its first flight. And this is just the beginning.

In the midst of this hectic activity, whenever I manage to find a quiet moment to reflect on these strange turns in my career path, I am astounded. What first looked like a disaster now looks like an amazing new adventure. I am part of a bootstrap startup for what promises to become a worldwide enterprise. I am confident this aircraft will fill a void. I am sure it will soon replace a myriad of other aircraft, currently serving the smaller airports of the world, with new, economical, comfortable, high-tech jet planes.

Still, I am a pilot. As far as I can tell, my new career opportunities will not involve aviating. Every six months I keep my appointment with the medicos. I want to build a timeline that might finally convince the authorities to let me have my license back. I hope that my heartbeat, though still a little wonky, will prove to be stable. Maybe it will even return to normal, or at least so I hope.

But it doesn't. Apparently, I am doomed to wonky. Along the way, I have met with a wide spectrum of medically-qualified specialists. They often express opinions about my desire to get back into the flight deck. Those who support me usually enjoy flying, and they usually agree. Once the evidence establishes that my symptomatic heart issues are stable, I should be safe to fly again. Other doctors, fearful of flying, usually express a negative opinion. They generally hold to the idea that, by even walking *near* an airport, I pose an unknown hazard to aviation safety. Yes, I'm exaggerating—but not by much. When fear grips our thinking, we are prone to project those fears into other activities and endeavors.

Finally, the day arrives. I've been off the line for nearly four years. My original lung symptoms, revealed by x-ray exams, immediately cleared up with treatment. My heart issue has proved to be completely stable by a long series of EKG tests. I have remained otherwise asymptomatic. I have puffed into tubes, run on treadmills, raced madly on bicycles to nowhere, been scanned, prodded, poked, flooded with radioactive isotopes and photographed from more angles than I thought possible. Now all I need is a doctor with the expertise and courage to come to a conclusion about my condition.

To this end, I manage to set up an appointment with the head honcho at Montreal's premier heart clinic, recognized as a world-class institute. I'm sitting quietly, hopefully, in a comfortable office chair before an unremarkable wooden desk. I am encouraged by how this physician apparently hangs his self-worth on something less ostentatious than an impressive executive desk. After a short interview, he browses through my thick medical file and finally looks up.

"I'd rather fly with you than any other pilots out there. I have a good picture of your cardiac situation, and it doesn't worry me. It's all those pilots out there whose hearts I don't know about who concern me more."

"Would you be willing to put that into writing?" I ask.

He was. And he did. And that was the nail in the coffin of the case against me—the medical opinions which had kept me from flying for nearly four years. I'd been through so many medical tests over those years that I was beginning to feel I'd earned at least an associate medical degree. One way or another, I am acquiring a medical education, even if I often felt more like a lab rat than a human patient. I'm ecstatic that this trial-by-doctors may soon come to an end.

It has taken a long time to build up the evidence allowing Transport Canada's head medico—who holds the bureaucratic authority over my license—to sign off and send me back to work. But it has happened at last. I'm back in the mill. It's time for more re-training. I'm going to resume my life as a pilot.

My airline status is quickly re-activated. The company has a new airliner in service—the Airbus A320. And now here I am, rounding off another circle, back where I started—only, different.

24

Sojourn

✈ ✈ ✈

If your life is like mine, parallel stories are always unfolding together and often intertwining in mysterious ways. So far, I've been sharing career-related tales. Now, two major storylines intersect—my professional journey and my spiritual journey.

This book is subtitled "a pilot's journey," so fear not—I'm not about to take a major turn to matters of faith, religion and spirituality. I tried to never inflict my own beliefs on flight deck colleagues, and I'm aiming not to do that to you either. This is not to say I have any problem discussing such things. In fact, I enjoy it. But now I only need to touch briefly on a conflict that arose between my career and my faith, and the strange way it resolved.

Have you ever experienced an emotional or spiritual crisis? I'm talking about a time when you longed to know if your life has any meaning or purpose—if the inevitable trials and pains are worth the struggle. In my journey, such an event occurred when I was 18 years old and began attending university.

It was 1969 and the news of the day was the Vietnam War. As a Canadian, I was not susceptible to a military draft, but our universities were politically active and full of unrest, almost as much as campuses south of our border. Like our American neighbors, we wrestled over the troubling issues of war in far-off Southeast Asia. One issue confronting Canadians was American "draft-dodgers." Should we offer them asylum or ship them back to "face the music" of their own justice system?

Our nightly news featured scenes of idyllic Vietnamese jungles suddenly erupting into napalm-fired infernos, defoliated landscapes and the constant, terrifying stream of dead American soldiers returning home in bodybags. Young men my age were off-loaded from C-130 Hercules aircraft and arranged on airport **tarmacs**. These images seared into my brain.

I could make no sense of it. I had been raised a "good Christian kid" and had a typically immature childhood faith that proved to be inadequate. My faith was not sufficiently robust to handle these on-slaughts of apparent national insanity.

I looked at the surrounding madness and asked myself how the kind, loving Jesus of my Sunday School lessons could permit such carnage in *his* world? I concluded that there is no God. I began to live my life accordingly, throwing off many of the constraints I carried from my immature belief system.

Flash-forward a few years. I am a young father of two children. Our little family has moved a couple of times to follow my career as an airline pilot. My wife and I have struggled to make a marriage work within the challenges of the era of "free love" and the turbulence of the 1960s and 70s. We failed. The marriage failed.

I have lived through the stress of divorce. Now, in order for my ex-wife to pursue her education and professional goals, and to prevent my children from becoming strangers to me, I move to Edmonton while keeping my job in Winnipeg. I commuted.

In the 1980s, long-distance commuting by airline pilots to a company base in a different city was a strange concept. Only a few rogue pilots dared buck the general expectations. The unwritten rule required pilots to live at their home bases.

I knew commuting was pushing the envelope with my employer, so I lived under constant pressure. I could never miss a work assignment due to commuting. I found an affordable place to stay in Winnipeg the night before each week's flight *pairing*. I had to check flight schedules and passenger loads constantly because I was commuting standby. I could only get on flights with empty seats. The vagaries of weather, flight cancellations and a limited number of flights available each day added layers of stress as I strove to ensure I could get to work on time.

After a couple of years of this lifestyle, I was emotionally on the edge and ripe for another crisis. I couldn't keep all the balls in the air any longer and was nearing a breaking point. Under the usual strain of both my professional and personal life—along with commuting, dealing with the sale of the family home, the death of a marriage and all the associated dreams and expectations—my world was reeling.

This crisis, and the desire to find meaning and purpose in life, ultimately drove me to re-examine my concepts of God, faith and religion. I once held to a childhood faith in a supreme Creator, which proved inadequate to the challenges of the real world. But now I realized this faith was only based on things others told me. I had never examined faith for myself with the same tenacity and adult commitment I applied to other important aspects of my life—such as how to fly an aircraft. So, I resolved to re-examine the belief in God in general—and Christian faith in particular—with greater effort and sincerity.

The medical issues and the four years I was grounded arrived amidst these spiritual struggles. Once my medical problems were resolved and I was scheduled for re-training as a first officer on the Airbus A320, I received my schedule for my flight simulator course. My stomach tightened.

Just a couple of years earlier, while medically grounded, I became involved with a church that taught a strict interpretation of the Jewish laws in what Christians call the Old Testament. They believed that a relationship with God required religiously keeping the Ten Commandments, and most of all the fourth commandment to "keep the Sabbath Day." The Jewish Sabbath begins on our modern calendars each Friday at sunset. During a Canadian winter, sunset can be as early as four o'-clock in the afternoon!

A conflict immediately arose between the training schedule and my new beliefs. Nervously, I made an appointment to visit the director of the training department to explain my predicament and to ask for special dispensation. Could my schedule be altered to accommodate my beliefs? I knew several people in this church who have given up or lost lucrative careers because of their religious convictions, so I was understandably concerned.

As it turned out the company was willing, though not very happy, to accommodate my beliefs. I was lucky to be employed by a federally-chartered Canadian company, subject to laws guaranteeing freedom of religion. This is an act of grace enshrined in our constitution and something I cherish.

Consequently, I was never certain whether the cooperation I received was a function of our nation's constitution or a personal favor granted by my employers. Were they extending a favor out of kindness, willing to extend me a favor and not punish me for my beliefs, or did they merely want to reward me for being (until now) a good employee—or some combination of all these factors? I don't know. But I am deeply grateful that despite the disruption to others training with me, my request was granted. I am equally thankful that my fellow trainees and instructors took my strange religious request in stride and didn't give me flak for the inconvenience I caused. I still wish today I had expressed my gratitude more clearly to my employer and colleagues.

Now here was the blatant irony of the situation that helped me move beyond the rule-keeping, moralistic tenants of this Sabbath-keeping religion. These company officials, according to my church, were judged as "outsiders," not yet under the umbrella of the "one true faith." Yet they were extending *grace* to me. Pure and simple grace. And in my religious blindness, I was acting as if *I* was the holy one, closer to God than they were.

Thankfully, since then, I have grown—been *uplifted*—into a different view about who was truly expressing the nature of God in this situation. I wonder at a Creator who is not above using irony to point out the shortcomings of my beliefs, and my need to move on.

Through all this, I learned how hard it is to step out from the crowd and live by paradigms and beliefs that are socially unpopular, especially when they might cost you a career. Living a counter-cultural life is challenging and sometimes, downright frightening. We all want to fit in, whether we admit it or not. How we go about choosing to fit in, and with whom, seems to be the critical factor.

I learned how easily we (or at least I) can buy into off-track—even cultish—beliefs and behaviors. What proclivities in me made this possible? Why did I go from one ditch (my youthful declaration that "there is no God") to another (legalistic Sabbath-keeping)? How do I ensure I don't fall prey to the same things again?

Within a year or two, my worldview was shaken once again—I came into a new sense of freedom—a new understanding of God's love and our role as humans in sharing that love with others. It was a game-changer.

In these later years, I look back and see how my entire worldview shifted dramatically. I like to think that it has been an onward, upward journey toward the greater truths about how and why we all exist in this amazing, breathtaking and all-too-temporary experience called *life*. I sometimes like to start conversations by asking, "Over the past couple of decades, have you ever had to make any major changes in your views of life, the universe and everything?"

Socrates once said, "The unexamined life is not worth living." I don't know if I'd go so far as that, but I can certainly agree that a self-examined life brings an ongoing feast of surprises, pains and opportunities to grow!

So, while all this was going on in my personal and spiritual life, my professional life was moving on as well. I soon finished the Airbus flight simulator course and successfully passed the flight test. The inspector stamped my license with a new endorsement for an EA32 Aircraft type, and back I went for line pilot training. I wondered again at this ever-swirling spiral of life.

25

Take that, Chicago!

✈ ✈ ✈

First Officer's Log:
1990 / A320 / ORD (Chicago), Arrival Rwy 22R
(My Line Check Flight on the new plane)

The early A320s had a tendency to make firm landings. The landing gear legs were very stiff. Later modifications to the shock absorbers improved this—a little. That's my story and I'm sticking to it.

Airplanes are great ego-busters. Any pilot who thinks he or she has mastered landings is in for a bad surprise. A cagey old captain once rhymed, "Always remember, and never forget. Your next landing could be your worst one yet." He wasn't wrong.

This is my route indoctrination. It's my final series of flights on the A320 under the watchful eye of a supervisor captain from the base where I have been posted. The Training Center said I'm "good to go"—now I have to prove it. I'm flying from the first officer's usual seat on the right-hand side. My check-captain is doing the monitoring duties.

We left Toronto just one hectic hour ago and are now descending into Chicago. As usual, the airspace is busy, the radio alive with the non-stop staccato of short-clipped ATC clearances and pilot responses. The Arrival Controller is **vectoring** (directing) us into the lineup for landing on runway 22R. It's a quick arrival. I'm starting to squirm because I'm getting jammed into the "go-down/slow-down" problem. Jet airplanes are streamlined, so while descending it is almost impossible to decelerate. Anyone who has started running down a steep hill, then discovered they can't stop will get this.

So, now I'm struggling to keep our aircraft sliding down the required descent profile while wrestling with limitations of Airbus automation. As a safety feature, autopilots cannot capture a glide slope signal from above. We must get under the electronic slope, then ease into it from

125

below. This is a pain in the brain on today's steep, close-in trajectory. We're busy communicating with ATC and doing our checklists; hands are reaching quickly and efficiently around the flight deck, extending speed-brakes and flaps in a drive to stay bang-on our assigned speed. We've been vectored into a tight arrival slot within a long string of inbound aircraft, and we need to stay right in the center of it.

Meanwhile, a B757 is arcing in from the south, on our left, to take up the slot ahead of us. We have the proper separation for wake turbulence, which is important. The "fifty-seven" is notorious for its strong wing-tip vortices. We know there is another aircraft on our tail, a mere three miles behind us. I dare not let our speed sag below the assigned value until we arrive at the **final approach fix (FAF)**, which is located about four miles back from the runway.

At the FAF we make our next radio frequency change and check in with the tower controller. We've been maintaining 180 knots, as assigned. We now need to slow aggressively to 120 to get stabilized on the final approach segment. I call for the captain to extend more aircraft parts into the breeze, to create more drag. There is another flurry of hands as the wheels go down, the flaps extend another notch, we make our required checks and double-checks and get a word in edgewise to the tower. Chicago packs a lot of airliners onto these runways and it only works because we all know the routine. Go fast to the FAF. Slow as rapidly as possible to the landing speed. Land. Get off the runway. *Move!*

To make the landing a little more interesting, a nasty, gusty wind is howling across our runway from right to left. Usually, I'd add a few knots more speed to help counteract this crosswind. However, our ideal exit point from the runway into our ramp is only two-thirds along the short runway. I don't want to zoom past it.

Now I'm fighting with the automation again. The Airbus has its own way of doing things. During windy approaches, it wants to add several knots to our final approach speed in order to increase safety margins if the wind suddenly stops. I want 120 knots. The Airbus Gremlins are keeping it closer to 150. If we were the only airplane in the sky, this technique is fine. But today, the Boeing 757 ahead of us is getting a little too close for comfort. I choose to override Otto (autopilot) and make him do things my way. This forces me to look to the knobs and buttons inside the plane at a time when I need all my attention outside, ensuring we are playing nice with the other aircraft—sharing this approach.

My observation that I'm losing our spacing from the 757—getting out of our slot—is confirmed by the tone of the controller's voice. He asks us a second time to confirm we've slowed to our final approach speed. He too is obviously unhappy with the Airbus' proclivity for a higher approach speed. His words carry the coded message: "Stay back from the 757 or I'll have to make you pull up and fly a missed approach, which none of us wants. We're all busy enough."

I take hold of the joystick and click Otto off, calling for another "notch" of flaps. Now I can slow right down to the minimum approach speed. Things begin to settle down. In the top corner of my electronic displays, I notice the upper winds around us, changing to match the wind on the airport. The auto-thrust adjusts. I quickly look around the flight deck: the wheels are down, the checklists are complete. In all the activity and distraction, I can't recall if the tower controller told us "cleared to land," so I ask the captain to confirm this, and the captain confirms it. Yes, we have landing clearance.

A B737 is taking off on another runway, crossing through the intersection with our runway. They move a lot of airplanes through tight spaces at O'Hare. It's hard not to be distracted. Chicago controllers are masters at this, I reassure myself. Just play along. Do our part correctly.

I continue, knowing the 737 will clear our intersection—just in time. We come bouncing and rocking over the buildings near the airport. The gusting surface winds are deflecting and swirling vertically into turbulent eddies.

Up ahead, I see the 757 is turning off at the far end of our runway, but his tail is slow to clear the landing path. This is closer than I like for runway separation. But this is Chicago. It's doable. It's not unusual here. Most importantly, I know that his distant exit point is well beyond my planned turnoff. I have no intention of rolling that far down the runway. Even if I should need to, at his present speed, the 757 will be clear just before our wheels touch down. Chicago controllers are masters at this, I reassure myself yet again. Play along. Do our part correctly.

The captain calls, "Minimum, runway in sight." Then I respond, "Landing." The visibility is not an issue today, but this coded call is part of the "incapacitation drill." That means my response confirms for him that I'm alive and still aware enough to land the plane. I haven't quietly suffered a brain aneurysm or slipped into a diabetic coma. Now he knows he won't need to fight me for the controls at 200 feet above the runway—unless I really scare him by messing up.

The digits on the radio altimeter flash larger and become more pronounced. Our planet is very near. I should pay particularly close attention. The computerized voice calls, "Fifty," and I start **"de-crabbing."** That is, I make a final adjustment of the aircraft heading with the runway. Until now, I've been aiming the aircraft several degrees right of the runway track to keep us flying along the extended centerline. Now it's time bring the fuselage, landing gear and runway centerline all into alignment.

The auto-voice continues in a commanding tone, "Thirty, Ten, Retard, Retard." This last call is not a politically incorrect insult, but a redundant reminder to close the thrust levers. We're rocking in the turbulence, our wings suddenly taking small dips to one side, then the other. I'm pulling the thrust back and thinking, now is a good time to flare. Just before I begin easing the nose up, lowering the right wing a tad to cancel the crosswind drift and pushing the left rudder pedal to keep straight, I hear a sound like the captain sucking air between his teeth. Then KABOOM! The entire airplane shudders. The runway rises up and strikes us hard on the wheels.

The flight deck shakes and rattles as the main wheels, so far behind and below us, grab the pavement. The nose is wrenched around. The laws of momentum, drag and torque accomplish what I was about to do, lurching us sideways to align with the runway. In response to my late pull on the joystick, the nose rotates upwards. This momentarily transfers some weight off the wheels back onto the wing. Then, the wing spoilers spring up, killing our lift—just as they are meant to. I sense a sinking lurch of the airplane, distinct from my own sinking feeling in my gut. The whole weight of the craft drops violently, compressing the long, chrome landing gear struts.

Then the autobrakes cut in, slamming the nosewheel onto the runway with another loud thump before I'm expecting it. My reflex to prevent this is too late, and the nosewheel ricochets into the air again momentarily. I am causing a PIO (Pilot Induced Oscillation).

I relax my death grip on the side-stick. The nosewheel drops back onto the pavement a second time. I fumble to deploy the thrust reversers, but it doesn't matter because by the time they're working, the brakes are slowing us down—too much. We're almost stopping before our turnoff. I can imagine the airliner behind us closing rapidly.

"Better kick the autobrakes off," the captain warns. As we slow, they seem to be grabbing even harder, throwing me against my shoulder straps. I have to slide my feet up to the brakes, which are at the top of each rudder pedal. But my shoes don't slide easily on the non-skid coating. I quickly release my pressure on the rudders for a moment, to lift my feet into the tops of the pedals. I need to pulse them—to tell "Otto-Brake" to take the rest of the flight off. The airplane swerves right, then left while I get my feet rearranged. The auto-braking goes away. It feels like we're surging ahead again. I convince myself this is just an illusion and stop myself from reacting to it.

Then the controller is telling us, "No delay clearing at Charlie. Traffic on short final..."—so I add a shot of power to keep our taxi-speed up. I move my right hand from the joystick to the nosewheel steering control to carve us around the corner into the taxiway. The captain calls, "I have control," and I gladly release these instruments of mayhem I've been flailing away on.

I quickly switch the radio onto the busy ground control frequency to negotiate clearances across the taxiways and into the ramp area, immediately ahead of us.

The captain calls for the after-crash check, with a bit of a chuckle in his voice, which I am truly grateful for. By his tone of voice and use of that word "crash," I realize this isn't his first rodeo. It's not his first experience of a first officer's rusty landing techniques.

While I work my way through the various panels, chanting and re-configuring switches and levers, the flight deck door swings open. In staggers our purser, Razzer Randy. He is grasping his neck, with both hands, like a brace. "Take that, Chicago!" he gasps, then breaks into a big laugh and punches me on the shoulder. We've flown together many times before. "Don't worry chief," he adds. "I told the passengers you're a great pilot, just a lousy driver!" He laughs again. "And you owe us lunch in Chicago; we had to re-stow a half-dozen oxygen masks." Then he leaves, still laughing.

I ask the captain if I should log the arrival as a heavy landing. This would require a maintenance inspection before the next flight. He shakes his head, "No. I won't mention any names, but that wasn't even the roughest landing I've seen on the Bus. You'll have to drop more masks than that to scare me. But of course, you—as in *not me*—will be standing at the door, saying goodbye to the passengers."

Soon, I'm doing just that, with as big a smile as I can muster, as if to say, "Heck, that was one of my best landings ever!" I grin and endure the mainly humorous comments from the deplaning passengers about how I should work on that driving technique. And there's always a few passengers who know some bad-landing jokes—and aren't afraid to use them. "Was that a landing or were we shot down?" Ha! No, I never tire of that one.

I keep grinning. "Thanks for flying with us. Come back again as soon as you've recovered. There's more where that came from." Despite the embarrassment of a bad landing, there's another feeling I'm experiencing. The banter feels good. I'm immersed in the give-and-take of line operations once again. It feels good to be back.

The next day, I'm standing in the local grocery store checkout. I notice the cashier is wearing a big round badge declaring: "Just Learning. Please Be Patient." I smile and imagine myself greeting passengers for my next flight, wearing a similar badge.

26

MENTORING MOMENTS

One of the line-captain's accepted duties is to guide and mentor new first officers, grooming them through experience for the day when they'll advance to their own captain's job.

Other than encouraging captains to share the flying duties with the first officers, the company didn't provide much in the way of specific instructions on how to accomplish this on-the-job training.

As first officer, I encountered every imaginable style of mentoring. To many of these gentlemen, I owe a huge debt of gratitude. It was a joy to work with captains who exemplified all the best ways of "being a captain." From some, I learned the value of constant attention to detail. From others, the value of humor and a team-oriented approach. From others still, the importance of striving for high standards while encouraging the same from those around.

I remember Captain Last as a true mentor. He became a kindly guide into the mysterious ways of captaining an airliner. He involved me in flight deck decisions. Most significantly, when he said, "You have control," he meant it.

I remember a couple of mentoring moments in particular:

"Are you going to fly us straight into those thunderstorms, or what?" Captain Last was staring at me over his sunglasses, smiling. He waved his right hand in the general direction of the weather radar images on his screen, then towards the huge, billowing clouds filling the view out our front windshield.

I suddenly realized that subconsciously, I'd been waiting for directions from him regarding the route he wanted to follow, to avoid the hazards ahead. I'd fallen asleep at the decision-making switch. Even though it was my turn to fly—meaning I was to choose our flight path—I had unwittingly abdicated my responsibility.

But Captain Last was having none of it.

Many captains gave their first officers latitude in other areas of managing the flights but then reverted to a directive form of commanding when navigating around these always dangerous behemoths of bad weather.

Over the years, when I'd flown with such captains, I had presented my plans for navigating through a stormy region, only to have them struck down. "No, go this way." So today, when Captain Last voiced this question, I realized I'd lapsed into a bad habit of not bothering to make my own analysis. I'd been unconsciously waiting to be told what to do.

That's the easiest way to get through life anyway—right? Just waiting for instructions. Not bothering to form our own opinions. What's the point in doing all that work, only to have your ideas summarily struck down and rejected?

The problem is, this attitude leads to detachment and complacency. It can become career suicide. Under the advancing concepts of **CRM** **(crew resource management)**, even in its infancy in the 1970s and '80s, co-pilots were expected to have an opinion and express it. Two brains truly are better than one, as long as there's a healthy relationship between them.

I snapped out of my complacency, leaned forward and began studying the storms ahead. It was fairly obvious which way to navigate around the cells ahead. As it turned out, Captain Last agreed—or at least he didn't disagree. I reached up to the auto-flight control panel and made the necessary heading change, hoping my choices would turn out to be good ones.

From that day on, I resolved to always be busy, plotting my own solutions to the ongoing flight issues. I tried always to be ready to give an answer when asked and to support it with appropriate evidence and logic. I also made the effort to express my opinions, when I thought they were helpful, but with a loose grasp on the non-critical, non-safety-oriented ones. I might express what was on my mind with a direct statement, but I also learned the power of a question. Asking my fellow pilot, "What do you think about this...?" was often a more effective way to finding the best solution as a crew.

If the captain liked what I said and approved my ideas, I felt an immediate responsibility for the outcomes. If he dismissed them for some reason, I could just let it go. After saying my piece, and providing there were no glaring safety-related issues at stake, my role was to focus on making his plan work. No emotional angst. No need to be right. No drama over decisions that had no immediate implications for safety.

There is no better way to develop good decision-making skills than to make decisions. And then to implement them—and deal with the consequences.

"Why don't we just put the trim in the green band and go without the numbers?"

Captain Last was staring at me over the top of his sunglasses—again.

We were stuck on the ramp at **LAX**, caught in a frustrating delay and waiting for load data. Our pushback and initial taxi-out had been routine. We had a short distance to taxi to our departure runway, so I got onto the company frequency as soon as possible after our engines were started to request our weight and balance numbers from the local company station. But despite my best attempts, including verifying that our number two radio was actually working, I was getting no response.

Things suddenly got complicated. We had to rapidly alert LAX ground control that we did not yet "have our numbers." We would not be ready to take off in the normal sequence. The controller had to quickly assign us a different route around the maze of taxiways—to get us out of the lineup and let other flights keep moving. Finally, she got us parked out of the way, and Captain Last set the brakes while I kept trying to get our takeoff numbers.

I used our datalink system to contact our Toronto flight dispatch center. Ironically, we could pass messages across thousands of miles with relative ease, but couldn't talk to our agent in an office just a few hundred feet away. As our fuel quantity continued ticking down for several more long minutes, we learned that the Los Angeles agent had just plain forgotten us and gone home! We couldn't even get our precious numbers from Toronto via the datalink because apparently, the local agent was so keen to get home he had failed to relay the key data to our centralized load-control center.

Captain Last and I both shrugged, feeling frustrated. We were now stuck—wasting time, burning fuel and losing money for our employer—as our projected arrival time at our destination fell further and further behind schedule.

That's when Captain Last posed his question, "Should we just put the trim in the green band and take off anyway?"

The numbers we were waiting for, called the "load figures" or "weight and balance data," are an important ingredient in every pre-flight preparation. All aircraft must always be properly balanced in order to be controllable. Our manuals give specific limits for where the center of gravity can fall, and this must be verified for every flight. This is the not merely the law; it is a basic tenet for staying alive.

For all aircraft, all the time and everywhere, the rule is clear: no numbers, no go. These numbers told us where to set our longitudinal balance—our trim indicator—within the green takeoff band, ensuring that we could expect a familiar response in the flight controls as we began lifting the nose for takeoff. A properly set trim meant there would be no sudden surprises. The nose of the plane wouldn't suddenly try to overrotate, nor would there be an unusually hard pull required on the yoke.

On a large airliner with several fuel tanks, cargo-holds and long passenger cabin, there's a lot of data that must be gathered and processed to ensure we have an accurate estimate of our balance. We also need to confirm that the maximum weight of the aircraft is within limits. *No numbers—no go.*

The system usually works smoothly and reliably, despite the complexities. But on this day, we were waiting for "the numbers," hoping our absent-minded agent was on his way back to **LAX** and not hung up in traffic on Interstate 405.

Our loading procedures had been developed over several decades to ensure ahead of time the aircraft was loaded properly. Consequently, the final check of our numbers had almost become a formality. The chances that the aircraft balance would be dangerously out of range were extremely low.

I thought about a famous takeoff by a B727 from Danang, Vietnam near the end of the Vietnam war a few years earlier. That aircraft had made an emergency takeoff—an escape actually—every nook and cranny filled with people fleeing the North Vietnamese army. The 727's rear air-stairs and cargo doors were still hanging open, and even the wheel wells were crammed with people. I'm pretty sure these pilots gave no thought to waiting around for official weight and balance numbers as bullets whizzed past the flight deck. That aircraft got airborne.

Captain Last was still staring at me over the top of his sunglasses—waiting for my answer.

"Well, yeah, if someone was shooting at us," I said, "I'd be all for getting the heck out of here. But otherwise, unless you want a couple of weeks off without pay, courtesy of the company and aviation regulatory authorities, I guess we should wait."

The law is the law and in this case, it was very clear. There was no gray area. There were no alternate procedures we could apply to safely find a workaround. Captain Last nodded. We waited.

I was never sure if he'd been serious about taking off without numbers, or was just testing me, seeing what my reaction would be. Eventually, the numbers came and they were right where they should be. We left routinely and were even able to regain some of our lost time en route. And no one—at least no one in our flight deck—got any disciplinary days off. As for our colleague in the LAX ramp office, I never did hear the full story of why he forgot us and went home.

We were on the downwind leg at Montreal (**YUL**) and there were several other planes on final approach, stretching east of the airport for several miles. It looked like we would be flying downwind for many miles yet, waiting for a spot to be turned back towards the runway.

Captain Last calls for me to extend the first notch of flaps so he can slow us down. "No need to fly any faster in the wrong direction than necessary," he says.

"You're the captain," I replied. I was trying to be a little humorous, reflecting that this early extension of flaps was a small deviation from the standard way of flying our approaches.

"What does that mean?" he smiled back at me as the flaps were extending. I glanced up. Captain Last was staring at me over the top of his sunglasses—again.

"Do you mean that you'd let me turn 90 degrees north, right now?" I was caught off guard. I hadn't meant much by my comment, but I'd learned by then that Captain Last was a thoughtful person—he constantly examined ideas and the words we use to express them.

I hesitated for a moment, thinking. My job as first officer was always about helping the captain do his job. But there were limits to this. Last was forcing me to consider these limits more closely. If at any time I thought he was operating unsafely, perhaps flagrantly violating the SOPs, then my task switched from that of an assistant to a resistant. As co-pilot, I was charged to follow the captain, but only as the captain followed his directives, laws, guidelines and procedures specified in his job description.

This dual role—as helper but constant judge and critic— makes the captain/ first officer relationship one of the most interesting and sometimes troublesome relationships anywhere. Having two qualified pilots working together produces a huge increase in safety—so long as they work together as a cohesive unit. This was the heart of the **CRM (crew resource management)** philosophy which was developing in airline training centers around the world at that time. Gone, supposedly, were the days when the captain was "god" and the first officer was there only to raise and lower the landing gear on command.

As all these thoughts swirled within my mind, I finally replied, "Well, I'd certainly try to discourage you from doing that."

"Glad to hear that!" Last said.

Captain Last made no attempts to jeopardize our safety that day, and I didn't need to resist him or fight for control of the aircraft. Instead, as always happened when I flew with him, I came away with something more to think about. In this case, our roles on the flight deck and what it truly means to captain an airliner.

27

That Time You Said "Oops" and Other Stories

✈   ✈   ✈

"I was never afraid of flying until you became an airline pilot."

"Gee, thanks Mom," I said.

"I mean it. I used to think airline pilots were special. Now I realize anyone could be up there flying my plane."

I loved my mother's humorous observation. At least I hope it was humorous. To her, I'd always be that clumsy little boy she worried would never learn to tie his own shoelaces. Now apparently, someone had made the terrible mistake of letting me at the controls of a multi-million-dollar airliner full of passengers. It shook her confidence.

"Now I'm definitely going to need that pre-flight drink before I travel," she said.

When I became an airline pilot, my mother was forced into the realization that airline pilots are not special. We are not infallible. We are pretty normal. Though we are continuously trained and tested and checked and prodded to maintain a very high standard this is done for a reason. There's also a reason that we have two pilots at the controls. We are only human after all and we make mistakes. We sometimes have memory lapses and hopefully, our co-pilot will notice and correct us in time to prevent accidents. *Here are a few of my favorite tales of forgetful pilots* (just don't show these to my mother.)

Parking Problems

I used to enjoy working with Captain Bernie. He kept the flight deck environment light-hearted yet professional. His wife usually chauffeured him to work, especially in the early years of his career when they had a small income and only one family car. Anyway, late one wintry night after a four-day trip, he arrived back from his flight cycle and, as usual, hurried down to their rendezvous point in the passenger pick-up zone in front of the terminal building. He waited. And waited. And waited. This was before cell phones. And began fuming that she was late—very late. Finally, freezing cold, frustrated and angry, he stomped over to the cab stand and hired a taxi for the ride home.

He stormed into the house and began a verbal tirade about his spouse's apparent failure in the family transportation department. Finally, when he paused for breath she asked, "Are you finished?" He remained silent. Then she calmly informed him, "You took the car to the airport."

Captain Fortine

Flight tests are always hard on the nerves. It's intimidating to have your boss working next to you in close quarters, judging every action and decision you make throughout a flight, from the way you communicate with other crew members to the technical details and understanding you display operating the aircraft. But I always felt a little more at ease when my **check rides** were scheduled with Captain Ren Fortine.

Ren was an ex-military pilot and I easily pictured him as the prototypical young gallant World War II fighter pilot, sporting a white silk scarf and leather bomber jacket, steely blue eyes turned towards the skies and a slight grin pulling at his lips. He was a gentlemen-of-gentlemen, a man representing a bygone era of chivalry. In his role as Chief Pilot, he expressed a genuine sense of care for "his pilots." Our flight manuals said that "a check flight should leave the candidate a better pilot, able to carry out the job with growing confidence and ability ..." No one made these words ring true better than Ren. Over the years Ren developed into an airport legend, due especially to a couple of incidents that revealed how even the "best-of-the-best-of-the-best" remain human. I believe Ren enjoyed a good laugh at his own expense and may have been the original source for the stories about him.

More Parking Lot Blues

Captain Ren Fortine had a houseful of guests staying with him over the holidays. They were heading back to Toronto on the same day he was going to work. Naturally, Ren drove them to the airport. They were running a little late when his car lurched to a stop in front of the Winnipeg airport departures door. Everyone piled out of the car and Ren hurried inside to grab a luggage cart while his friends unloaded the baggage. He helped them check in at the front counter then directed them towards the correct gate. They joked about having their captain in full uniform ushering them through the terminal.

Now Ren was getting even later for work, so he rushed up to the flight planning center and met up with his first officer, who had completed the flight planning details. The two pilots hurried off to their flight and departed on time.

Minutes later, as their DC-9 was climbing through twenty thousand feet, Ren remembered that he'd left his car sitting in front of the terminal building, doors open, engine running.

A Stitch in Time Saves DC-9

Captain Ren Fortine was an excellent pilot and well-liked by his peers, but he was known to occasionally forget things. Like the day he arrived in the flight planning center, dropped his satchel against the far wall in 'luggage row,' and then flipped the top open to grab his planning charts. But instead of the expected manuals, he discovered his wife's *Singer* sewing machine. He suddenly remembered that he'd bought a spiffy new work bag the previous week and his wife had claimed his old one for her sewing room.

A hurried phone call ensued and the correct bag was soon delivered to the airport. In the meantime, Ren was kept busy with requests from his amused colleagues to re-sew loose buttons or reinforce a uniform seam.

Location, Location

Captain Ren Fortine was conducting the last few check flights with a new first officer assigned to his base. The flights were going well. This was the last day. They were having a relaxed conversation during cruise when Ren glanced over the nose of the plane to see the city of Regina about to pass under the plane. "Could you please make a short announcement to the passengers to update them about our ETA and the weather and let them know we're just about over Regina," he said.

"Regina?" the first officer said. "We're supposed to be landing in Regina."

A hurried descent soon followed.

Sky-Caps

This story isn't about forgetfulness so much as playfulness. One evening after a long day's flying with Captain Fortine, we were standing on the curb outside the terminal building, waiting for our hotel shuttle-bus to take us to a much-needed overnight rest.

A cab sped up, lurched to a halt and a harried family spilled out. Dad began slinging the luggage from the trunk onto the sidewalk at our feet. "Get these over to the United Airlines counter right away—we're late for our flight." He had obviously confused us with the airport porters—the *Sky-Caps*.

Captain Ren, instantly grasping the mistake and enjoying the opportunity for humor, grabbed the two largest suitcases and hustled them through the revolving doors. What could I do? I grabbed the other two. We deposited them onto a luggage cart as the family scurried up. Someone suddenly realized the error. There were red faces and laughter as Captain Ren refused to accept the tip. "Hey! I'll take that," I thought to myself. I was just recently off "flat salary"—a pilot's initial pay scale when wages are shockingly low—so I was only half-joking. We wished them good-flight and hurried back outside to catch our bus.

Without Your Pants

I should conclude these anecdotes by telling a couple about myself.

I was visiting my mother at her acreage west of Edmonton. Dad had passed away a few months earlier. She was still living at the country home they'd built together after his retirement. I knew she was going through a confusing readjustment—her first year alone after living with the same person for over 35 years.

So, when I had an Edmonton layover at the end of a flight pairing, rather than going downtown to the crew hotel, I arranged to visit her.

Because my next day's flight was a *"deadhead"* home, I stayed with her for a couple of nights. Later, as we drove the several miles from her country home to the Edmonton International airport, I took in the scenery. Around us were the familiar rolling hills and countryside where I'd grown up and learned to fly. I thought about my father's unexpected passing and how life can change dramatically yet somehow remain so much the same. It seemed like only yesterday that I'd flown over these same green hills and valleys, bouncing around the sky in a little Fleet Canuck, struggling to learn my craft. Now, just a few years later, I was living a thousand miles away in Winnipeg and working as a co-pilot on DC-9 airliners. I missed the long conversations I used to have with my Dad as I'd answer his questions about flying. He had worked as a locomotive engineer for many years and we enjoyed the similarities and differences between our jobs. Then one morning, he'd had an accident and was gone. It was all hard to connect.

As I said, this morning I was deadheading home, so I was wearing my street clothes. I'd packed my uniform away in my suitcase the night before. At least I thought I had. But just as we pulled up to the airport terminal building and parked, it dawned on me: I'd hung my uniform pants in her closet and they were still there.

"I forgot my pants at your place. Can you mail them back to me, please?"

She stared at me. "They let you fly those big airplanes but here you are, going to work without your pants? See why I'm afraid of flying?" She never let me forget about "that time you went to work without your pants."

That Time You Said "Oops"

A few years later my mother was traveling to Montreal where I was now based. She was coming to visit us for a few days. I'd arranged for her to travel on my flight because conveniently, it was the final day of a four-day trip which ended with a non-stop Edmonton to Montreal leg.

Before "9/11," in Canada we were allowed to have visitors into the flight compartment. Most pilots enjoyed the opportunity to meet some of our passengers and show them what happens in the pointy end of the plane. When the visitor was someone we knew and the weather conditions were favorable, we might even offer them the chance to view the landing from the observer's seat. Today, landing in Montreal, my mother is all buckled in and briefed on the flight deck procedures for visitors—things like no talking. Below 10,000 feet, the rule is that all flight deck communications are restricted to operational needs only. She obviously enjoyed the experience.

Later, as we were driving home, she turns to me and asks, "Why did you say, *'Oops'*? There are two people I never want to hear saying 'Oops'—my surgeon and my pilot. Why did you say 'Oops'?"

"What? When did I say 'Oops?' I don't remember saying 'Oops.'"

"While you were getting ready to land. You said, 'Oops.' Why did you say that?"

I thought back to the approach and landing. It had all been very routine. Then I recalled that as I was activating one of the airplane's computerized landing modes I had inadvertently tapped a wrong button. It wasn't a big deal. It simply meant I had to immediately select the correct switch beside it. But apparently, I'd said "Oops" and hadn't even noticed. But she had.

That was another thing I never heard the end of—"that time you said 'Oops.'"

PART 3
FOUR BARS

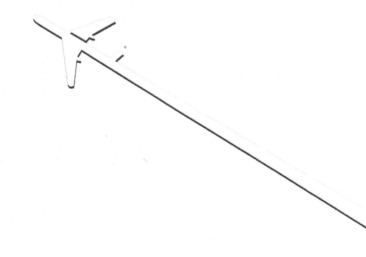

28

Captain, My Captain!

✈ ✈ ✈

The numbers again. Airline life always comes down to the numbers. Especially the numbers expressing time, which inexorably tick by until the day finally arrives. The new equipment bid is published and there is my name—at last—on the captain's list.

Each year, the airline laid out their plan for how many pilots they needed the following year. They took into account retirements, changes in the numbers and type of airplanes they planned to operate, anticipated passenger loads, flight frequencies and so on. Given the variables involved, the volatile nature of the airline industry and its vulnerability to changing economic conditions, the entire exercise must have been very complex.

These plans could change suddenly if economic indicators took a turn. Other factors, such as sudden changes to fuel prices, could affect the plan. So could regional wars, volcanic eruptions or large scale strikes by the dozens of employee groups within the industry. From air traffic controllers to pilots, to flight attendants or third-party companies that supplied fuel or loaded baggage—airlines are high-value targets, with significant effects on a country's economic output. If you shut down a large airline, you get everybody's attention.

Despite all these risks and the unforeseen problems that could render the plan obsolete—not unlike a pilot's flight plan—the airline's annual plan at least provided a reference to where we were, compared to where we hoped we'd be.

I stood at the flight planning counter, the loose-leaf binder opened to the projected captain's list, feeling a sense of accomplishment and anticipation. I had weathered all the previous years of training, checking, testing and unexpected medical problems. I had overcome each challenge. Finally, it all came together: seniority, time, the unavoidable pilot "expiration dates" (mandatory retirement), combined with airline expansion.

Finally, the hoped-for outcome—my name shuffled from near the top of the A320 first officer's list to near the bottom of the DC-9 captain's list. This was the funny stepladder of airline seniority—stepping back to a smaller, older aircraft for an upgrade in pilot status.

I looked forward to the challenge with just a little trepidation. As always, the voice of doom hovered in the background, assailing me with doubts: "What if you can't do it? What if you can't handle the added challenges and new responsibilities?" To silence these fiends, I immediately began cracking open the manuals. Over the next few months, if I was going to succeed in my long-sought-after quest to occupy the captain's seat, I would have to master the ropes of my profession like never before.

Nearly twenty years had passed since Bob McPlane's infamous "one-in-three" speech during my new-hire pilot course. I had come close to joining the ranks of those pilots who'd dropped out along the way. But I was still in the game. And my greatest tests as a pilot were soon to come.

Within a few months of the list being published, I was up to my eyeballs in a DC-9 reconversion course. I was shipped to Pittsburgh and the training facilities of USAirways. Then, after a couple of whirlwind weeks, more intense learning, flight tests and check flights, I was back on the line, flying officially as a DC-9 first officer. But now I was authorized to sit in the left seat to gain experience from that side of the flight deck. I was under the mentoring care of specific captains who had volunteered for this role.

There were a few familiar names on this list of captains who were so daring, crazy or in need of a few extra bucks that they'd willingly move to the right chair to monitor new captain candidates. They were expected to impart wisdom while keeping us out of trouble and protecting the passengers from us. I thought again of the grocery clerk's badge: "Be Patient, Please. I'm Just Learning."

At this stage, however, we were all experienced flyers. We just had to adapt to sitting on the other side of the cockpit. This meant relearning the visual cues out the front window and learning to swap hands. Now our left hand manipulated the yoke, while our right hand moved the throttles and the other flight deck controls. Before joining the airline, I'd flown from both left and right seats, so flying from the captain's seat was not an issue. But it was disconcerting to discover how hard finding switches, buttons and dials can be simply because my point of view had changed. All my habits of where to look and reach for every control and indicator were now wrong.

Most importantly, I now had to "play" at being captain. Suddenly, the burden of command was upon my shoulders—sort of. How much easier it had been to simply be a critic of captains as they managed flights. Now I was the one in the hot seat. Now I was expected to make the final decisions, knowing everyone around me was watching and judging me. No longer was I just throwing out my ideas, seeing if "they would fly"—if the captain would adopt them. Rather, I now had to consider the various ideas and input of others and act as final arbitrator and agent of which course to follow. The responsibility for all decisions now fell squarely upon me. Being the one in the hot seat, and not just an observer and critic, aroused in me an entirely new respect for those captains who had made it look so easy. Suddenly, it wasn't easy at all.

For this left-seat familiarization time, I looked to two or three individuals I'd flown with before and respected. I admired the way they ran their operations. They were confident enough to be relaxed in their command style. Their flight decks ran smoothly. Their relationships with everyone else who made the operation flow smoothly were invariably polite, friendly, professional and magnanimous. These other folks comprised such roles as air traffic controllers, mechanics, ramp personnel, refuellers, flight attendants, dispatchers, crew schedulers and more. Any Hollywood imagery of the lone wolf, uber-independent airline pilot, was revealed now as a strange fantasy. It takes a dedicated team to raise an airliner.

My chosen mentors never resorted to bouts of temper, intimidation or petulance when the operation was falling off the rails, as it often does. Whether due to bad weather, mechanical problems or the myriad of factors that affect daily operations of a large airline, these captains handled it. In my estimation, the best represented what the title "captain" should stand for. They represented what I hoped to emulate.

I logged the required left-seat hours as rapidly as possible in the next few months, trying to learn as much as I could about being *The Captain*. Soon, I was ready for the next critical step: doing it for real.

29

Lonely at the Top?

✈ ✈ ✈

They say it's lonely at the top. But maybe it doesn't have to be...

Captain's Log: Back on the DC-9

"So, what now, Captain?"

Our airplane has a snag and we haven't even left the gate. We discovered an unserviceable piece of equipment during our pre-flight preparations. We called for the mechanic to come and hopefully fix it. He hasn't been able to. Now, he's standing in the doorway of our flight deck looking directly at me.

The question hangs in the air, *"So, what now, Captain?"*

After many long years, I advanced in seniority from second officer on the B727, managing aircraft systems, onto my next assignment as first officer on the DC-9. I was thrilled to have my very own control column and window—although for the first six months, I probably only had time to look outside if I'd forgotten something. The FO's job on the DC-9 was the busiest post in the airline.

Our average flight leg was an hour or less on the intercity "milk runs." This is where I learned the art of all-weather instrument flying. We routinely flew to isolated northern and maritime airports in the morning, then on to the world's busiest terminals in the afternoon. We used every tool in our pilot's arsenal as we dealt with every type of approach. We could go from the seat-of-the-pants flying of a visual approach at an uncontrolled airport in northern Quebec to a fully-*vectored* instrument landing into Chicago's hectic O'Hare International. We routinely encountered the two extremes of airline flying in a single day.

While I concentrated on developing my piloting skills under the tutelage of master aviators, I also began to appreciate the captain's most important role as decision-maker. As a first officer, if a mechanic or flight attendant entered the flight deck with a tough problem requiring a "captainly" decision, I could simply rotate my head to the left,

149

waiting for our experienced captains to "earn the big bucks."

As a first officer, when left in charge of supervising the fuel loading or requesting a flight plan from our dispatchers, I was constantly aware I was speaking on the captain's behalf. We operate under the authority of the captain. I had to ensure any requests or decisions I made were expressing the captain's desires, not my own. This didn't have to be difficult since we are supposed to be "on the same page," working together.

Then one day, after I'd been on the DC-9 for a while, Captain Ren Fortine surprised me. It was a typical day with a typical problem that had just been dumped in his lap—as often happens, something to do with an unserviceable piece of equipment. The resulting dilemma wasn't clearly covered by the operations manual. With no clear-cut guidelines, it was the kind of decision that requires a healthy dose of common sense and good technical knowledge. Captain Ren surprised me when he turned and asked, "So what do you think we should do?"

"What?" I felt my brain slowly engaging another of its limited channels. It thought, "You're asking me what I think about this...?" I don't recall my response—probably something profound like, "Aaaah, wow, that's a tough one..." I soon realized that I enjoyed flying with Captain Ren and others like him because they expected me to contribute to the operation. Significantly, this was back in the days before **CRM (Crew Resource Management)** became the new standard. Some guys were just ahead of the pack.

Then, came the day when I found myself on the line—in command of my own airliner. The inevitable moment soon came when a mechanic entered the flight deck, looking for a decision to an obscure problem.

"So, what now, Captain?"

Perhaps my head reflexively snapped to the left, where all I saw was the reflection of my own face in the window.

"D'oh! Now what?"

I snapped my head back around to the right and addressed my first officer in my most captainly manner, "So, Number One. What are your thoughts on this?"

What a great stalling tactic. It not only made me look like one of those "cool" CRM-captains who values the first officer's opinion—it gave me time to think the problem through in more detail.

The realization dawned on me and sank in. As an aircraft commander,

I am not expected to be a one-man-band. In fact, just the opposite. The word *captain* implies there are other team members—I am merely at the head of this group, leading and coordinating their contributions toward a common goal. And of course, I am responsible for that final verdict—the flight operates under my authority.

Our team includes a first officer with valuable flying skills. She may have insight into things beyond my experience. And she probably remembers all the rules and SOPs better than I do. The first officer has the freedom to analyze situations apart from the pressure of carrying the final responsibility. She can be a less-involved monitor, able to add a second, sober opinion.

Our team also includes experienced **pursers** and flight attendants who are experts with people and cabin safety issues. They know the ins and outs of service, and what is needed for that end of the job. Our team includes highly motivated and professional mechanics—they understand the details of the aircraft much more deeply than I do. Our team includes lead station attendants who know how to properly load the cargo and monitor the outside servicing of the aircraft.

Our team includes professional flight dispatchers, the weight-and-balance technicians and extends to our air traffic controllers, flight service specialists, company gate agents and many others who provide the resources I will need to safely and efficiently accomplish each flight. I am not alone—not a one-man-band by any stretch of the imagination.

Realizing this took a lot of weight off my shoulders and allowed me to confidently seek and incorporate ideas from the whole team. Like the fictional Captain Picard on Star Trek's *Enterprise* (yes, Trekkies—I did say 'fictional'—sorry), I can picture myself assertively saying, "Ready room!" and leading my team off to a quiet conference chamber, where we will come up with the best response for any difficult situation.

But our flight decks have no such "ready room." So I make do with cramped quarters, often frustrating two-way radios and unreliable datalinks as I gather input to help to form good decisions. And of course, I rely on that all-important tactic of turning to the first officer or another resource person to ask, "What do you think we need to do here?"

But time doesn't always permit this level of consultation. Sometimes the captain must make unilateral decisions—subject only to my co-pilot's immediate responsibility to edit or correct or even challenge me—which does happen occasionally. Captains and first officers have a complex relationship. As Len Morgan, a retired airline pilot, once wrote, "Good captains and first officers go hand-in-hand—but not through the terminal building." A good team can function smoothly and become more than the sum of its parts.

Lonely at the top? It doesn't have to be. However, the captain must always remember to be *The Captain*.

30

Whoop! Whoop!

✈ ✈ ✈

When planets and airplanes collide, airplanes always lose.

Captain's Log: / DC-9 / approach into YYZ (Toronto)

In the 1970s someone invented a device to discourage pilots from playing this game of celestial chicken and the ***GPWS (Ground Proximity Warning System)*** was born. Ground Proximity Warning Systems work in conjunction with another instrument we call the ***Radio Altimeter***. This is an electronic altimeter that bounces radar signals off the earth and converts the returning signals into measures of distance. The GPWS computer monitors critical changes in this altitude and warns pilots of potentially inappropriate encounters with the mother planet. It has saved many aircraft and numerous lives.

Modern airliner flight decks are crammed with warning systems. Computerized voices, warning tones, various beeps and whistles, not to mention the continuous background chatter on our radios, can make our little room in the front a very noisy place.

The GPWS has the noisiest warning of all. When it figures that ground-contact is imminent, it erupts with a loud, rising-toned siren that sounds like, "Whoop! Whoop!" This is immediately followed with a loud voice commanding, "Pull Up! Pull Up!" A bright red light flashes in front of the pilot's eyes, accompanying the aural onslaught. There's no ignoring such a warning, which is entirely intentional. After all, running into the planet can ruin your whole day.

Flight decks can become a noisy microcosm of the same distractive environment most of us occupy each day. It can wear on a person. More than once, systems intended to make flying safer have confused and overloaded pilots, sometimes with disastrous results. We must then block out the information overload to concentrate on the most important thing—the one thing that will save our lives—flying the plane.

✈ ✈ ✈

We turn about a 10-mile final for Toronto's runway 23L and switch our radio to the final approach frequency to gather reports from flights that have just landed. We are always listening for these, but especially now because there is a cluster of small storms building rapidly and drifting into our approach path to the airport. Preceding flights have experienced only light rain, good visibility and little wind. The airplane immediately ahead of us says he will pass on his comments. We continue our approach, unaware of the mayhem awaiting us.

I've flown with First Officer Serge many times before. He's competent and well-experienced. He's flying this leg and I have no qualms letting him continue into this weather. During the pre-approach briefing, we discussed the problems it might cause and how we'll react. If we hit excessive turbulence or rain or other problems, we will immediately scrub the landing and go around. "Going around" means he'll set full power on the engines as he pitches the nose of the plane skyward and executes a maximum performance climb along the required path for overshooting this runway. Meanwhile, I will be retracting the wing flaps and landing gear and working the radio with ATC. If we encounter a worst-case scenario involving downbursts and windshear, we have an emergency drill specifically for that. We have reviewed and rehearsed it. We're ready.

For now, it doesn't look like this shower is going to be problematic. The flights ahead are reporting smooth air with only mild wind changes. But summer weather and rapidly-building cumulous clouds can change quickly.

As we cross the final landing fix five miles from the runway, we are 1000 feet above the ground. We are planning to descend to 500 feet above the ground and re-assess. I switch to the Pearson Tower frequency. The flight ahead just touched down. He says the visibility in the rain was adequate and there was no sign of excessive turbulence, downdrafts or wind shears. We still have a smooth ride as the first raindrops begin beating on our windshield. At our speed of 120 knots, the drops come at us horizontally rather than vertically. We are suddenly flying into a river of rain-streaks and they sound like a hail of steel pellets smacking the windshield and nosecone. The rain intensifies, flooding the windshield and the noise builds to a roar. I reach up to find the switch on the windshield wipers. There's nothing we need to see yet, but I don't want to be fumbling for it closer to the ground. I also want to know how well we can see. The combined roar of the rain and squeal of the wiper motors means we need to speak loudly to communicate.

The rain continues to intensify rapidly. With the wipers cranked up to full speed, making even more racket, our front window is a flood, splashing wildly as water is flung into the hurricane-force wind of our airspeed. It's almost like we're in a submarine. As we approach 500 feet above the ground, the rain intensity is heavier than I've ever seen. I'm hoping for signs of it easing so we can see out the front window. The previous flight did not report this much downpour. But the rain only gets worse. The windshield wiper motors squeal—the blades flash back and forth across the window, making slapping sounds as they sweep in small arcs across the glass.

I double check my math—Toronto airport is 570 feet high, so at 1070 feet on the barometric altimeter, we will be 500 feet above the terrain. This is confirmed by the radio altimeter, which assures ground clearance more directly.

Then we're at 500 feet. The rain shows no signs of abating. The shower is now a full-fledged storm. Our forward visibility is almost zero. I lean toward the first officer and give him the go-around call, "Let's get out of here—go around!" He happily complies, setting full power to the engines and calling, "Go around, flaps 15!"

I'm watching our instruments for confirmation that he sets full power accurately and raises the nose to at least 15 degrees above the horizon. When I see evidence that we're truly climbing, I call, "Positive rate." He acknowledges by calling, "Gear up." But before I can retract the wheels, the flight deck is filled with even more noise—loud, incessant GPWS warnings break out: "Whoop Whoop! Pull Up! Whoop Whoop! Pull Up!"

It takes me only two seconds to verify both vertical speed indicators, three barometric altimeters and two radar altimeters—all say we are climbing. Our altitude is more than 500 feet and the altimeter hands are winding rapidly clockwise. I remind myself: clockwise means increasing. This is good. It takes two more seconds for my heart to start beating again. I call loudly so Serge can hear me, "Positive rate confirmed. We're at least 600 feet above the terrain—do you agree?" Serge nods. I know he has also confirmed all the same indicators within the same two seconds and I have, and apparently, his heart is also still beating. He calls again for the landing gear retraction, almost shouting to be heard. I flip the gear lever up and the noise of the retracting nosewheel adds to the cacophony. Then we retract the flaps one more notch.

The noise is overwhelming. Rain smashes harder against the glass as our speed increases. The wipers whine and slap at the windows. Air-conditioning noises whoosh around us as the engines surge to maximum power.

Worst of all, the never-ending "Whoop Whoop! Pull Up! Whoop Whoop! Pull Up!..." is overloading my ability to think. The commotion below our feet from the nosewheel retracting, hitting the braking pad and grinding to a halt crescendos. The final thump of the gear doors closing drops the background tumult from deafening to a steady clamor.

I twist around in my seat looking for the circuit breaker that would kill the GPWS speaker. I desperately want to cut off that unnerving alarm. Then my overloaded brain echoes an old aviation adage that many instructors drummed into me over the years. It tells of the priorities of piloting: Aviate, Navigate, Communicate. We do things in that order. I return my attention to the instruments to confirm again that we are safely climbing and the earth is swiftly falling away beneath us. This GPWS is only a false warning and must be ignored, even while it continues to shout at us. It requires a Zen-like focus to block it out.

Meanwhile, I radio the tower to alert them of our go-around, then switch over to the departure frequency so another controller can issue further headings and altitudes. I wonder what ATC must be thinking—they are certainly hearing the warnings in the background of my transmissions. I'm also wondering how far back in the cabin the noise is penetrating. The flight attendants sitting just outside our thin flight deck door must be terrified, wondering if they are about to die. Should they be warning the passengers, "Attention! Brace for Impact!" or chanting "Hail Marys"? I'm also certain that the passengers in the first few rows are hearing this racket as well. But I'm too busy to talk to them right now.

I dial in the heading and altitude reminders as per our ATC instructions and ensure that Serge also hears them and is complying. I finally have a free hand, so I reach up and switch off the windshield wiper. I almost sigh as that noise ceases. Then after one last blast of rain on the window and one last "Whoop, Whoop! Pull Up!" we pop out of the rain shaft. The pandemonium of the last few moments abates and the flight deck suddenly goes quiet. As the FO eases off the power and captures the newly assigned altitude, we retract the last of the flaps. In near silence, we settle into a short low-level cruise to the west side of the airport.

"What was that all about?" Serge asks, speaking normally again.

"I'm not sure," I say. "Maybe it had something to do with the radio altimeter pinging off the heavy raindrops. Let's not take any chances that it will go off again." I pull out our quick reference card for the circuit breakers, find the coordinates of the offending system and by twisting around in my chair, I can just reach it. It is clearly labeled, but I check twice to make sure I've got the right one before pulling it. Another smaller and quieter annunciator light comes on with a subtler "bing," telling us that the GPWS system is now disabled.

I finally have time to make a brief announcement to the passengers. After landing, I will have a few more minutes to explain the false warning. If anyone near the front of the cabin was afraid of flying before this incident, I can only imagine what it will take to get them back onto another flight. Meanwhile, ATC is transmitting new headings to guide us back to the other end of the same runway. We complete a quick review of this new procedure, reset our radios and then I take a few seconds to give our company a call. I want to alert maintenance. If this GPWS unit is faulty, it will affect the dispatch of the aircraft for its next flight.

It had only been ten minutes since all the commotion began and we're back on the approach from the opposite direction in blue skies and sunshine. The rainshower has drifted away from the far side of the airport. Our second approach is normal and the touchdown is extra smooth thanks to the wet runway.

Silence really is golden.

31

A Flicker

✈ ✈ ✈

Captain's Log: / DC-9 / Departure
YUL (Montreal) to HOU (Houston)

Sometimes we get paid for things we don't do.

Aircraft are complex vehicles built to withstand the tremendous stresses inherent in flying at nearly 500 miles per hour. They routinely climb to the edge of the earth's atmosphere and back, then land at high speeds. Returning to earth requires a controlled dissipation of tremendous energy, momentum and—at least when I'm landing—vertical impact. Jet transports do this thousands of times over their lifetime. Sometimes things break. Tonight, it's a tire.

Our night departure from Montreal to Houston will be at least thirty minutes late because maintenance is changing one of our right-hand main wheels. The inbound crew reported a momentary fault in the anti-skid system. With slushy, slippery runway conditions like we have tonight, braking efficiency can change suddenly between patches of ice and bare pavement. This wheel probably locked up momentarily during the landing roll, and a patch of rubber tread suddenly burnt off the bottom of the tire. It's not uncommon, especially with older anti-skid systems such as the one on this DC-9. Along with changing our anti-skid control box, when I go outside to do the walk-around, I see our team of mechanics swarming around the wheels—they have the aircraft jacked slightly on the right side. The tire change is underway.

I walk carefully on the greasy ramp, checking the outside of the aircraft. Thankfully, the snow has stopped falling and our aircraft is "clean"—that is, there is no residual ice or snow clinging to the wings or fuselage. Once the tire is fixed, we should be ready to roll. We'll have a very short taxi to the active runway, which will allow us to get airborne quickly. Hopefully, we'll find opportunities to save a few minutes en route to Houston so we can arrive close to our scheduled ETA.

Soon, pushback is complete and the ground crew waves us off. I taxi slowly across the slush-covered ramp. Our taxi light helps us find our way as we move from the illuminated terminal building further into the dark night.

The first officer works through the checklists. The ramp and taxiways are slippery, but when I check the brakes, I am satisfied that the traction is reasonably good. I duck forward a little to glance up at the low, sodden cloud deck—barely above us. The cloud ceiling is so low that if we have a problem immediately after takeoff, we won't be able to return to this airport. We will be obligated to take whatever problem that might develop up the Rideau Valley to the Ottawa airport, where the ceiling is higher.

The checks completed, and our takeoff clearance received and acknowledged, I swing the heavy airliner onto the centerline of the runway and pause momentarily. Ahead of us, the asphalt surface is layered with residual slush. Tire tracks swerve away into the distance, evidence of flights that have recently departed ahead of us. From past experience, I can predict that as we progress further along into the region where few airplanes have operated, the pavement will be much slipperier.

By then we should be getting airborne. I don't want to think about how slippery it will be, should we have a problem and need to stop down there—but the fact that I briefly did so will be an important factor in what's about to happen.

With a full cabin and fuel for this long leg to Houston, we are near our maximum takeoff weight. The performance charts assure us we *should* have enough runway available to accelerate to our takeoff speed. Or if need be, using the maximum stopping ability of the plane—and presuming the anti-skid system does its job properly—we *should* be able to reject the takeoff and still stop within the runway confines. The operative word here is "should." Given the impossibility of accurately predicting the actual degree of runway friction, I would prefer not to put the numbers to the test.

I run the engines up to mid-power. We take one last reading of the instruments to ensure both engines are working normally, showing no signs of icing or slush contamination. I glance around quickly to ensure all the warning lights are out and we've forgotten nothing. Then, taking one last breath and exhaling it slowly, I smoothly push the levers to full takeoff thrust, allowing the first officer to make minor final adjustments while I turn my full attention out the front window.

Slowly, accompanied by the dull roar of two straining JT8D turbofans one hundred feet behind us, we begin to accelerate. The heaviness of the plane is evident by the low acceleration rate and the lumbering feeling as we roll over each bump and unevenness in the asphalt.

Gradually, the airspeed needle begins to wind clockwise, inching higher. Sixty knots. Seventy knots. Then the FO breaks the tense silence:

"The left **EPR (engine pressure ratio)** gauge flickered and came back up. It's at full power again."

In an airliner flight deck, there are dozens of dials, indicators and gauges. Any electronic or mechanical system can produce false readings. These *EPR* gauges have been known to flicker when they are partially clogged by ice or other debris. That is my first thought. It's probably just a gauge fluctuation—right?

I glance quickly to the center of the instrument panel and confirm what he's told me. Two perfectly normal-looking EPR gauges. So the needle flickered—what else could cause that? Again, I tell myself, it's probably just a minor problem with the indicator system itself—right? I return my attention out the windshield, glancing at the airspeed. It's climbing toward eighty knots.

But through hundreds of takeoffs over the many years I've been flying aircraft with EPR power gauges, I've seldom seen them flicker. Significantly, when I did see them flicker, there was a real problem. Perhaps an internal bleed valve failed to *sequence* properly. Or maybe we sucked a piece of ice or snow through the engine, damaging something.

I'm initially inclined to continue the takeoff—but then a quick rethink goes like this: the ceiling and visibility are marginal. Once we get airborne, we can't return to a quick landing here at Montreal. We'd have to divert to our takeoff alternate in Ottawa, where we'd face the complexity of an overweight landing.

Our speed is just now accelerating to 80 knots. At this point, a rejected takeoff isn't considered an emergency. Why not stop and have maintenance take a closer look, while that's still a simple matter? This thought flashes through my mind within seconds of the instant the first officer alerted me to the issue. Our speed continues to accelerate, about to exceed 80 knots—still a safe speed for us to stop from, even with the slippery runway conditions.

"Okay, well, let's have a look—Reject, Reverse." That's my coded call. It triggers a few other events. I pull the thrust levers to idle, then remove my hand so the first officer can deploy the reverse thrusters. At the same time, I'm applying light braking. There's no need to sling the passengers against their seatbelts or frighten them with a full-effort stop.

"Spoilers," the first officer reminds me. I've been distracted looking at the upcoming runway exit and neglected to pull back and latch the spoiler lever. I do it now, and it activates the system which disrupts airflow across the top of the wing, ruins any lift the wing is generating and keeps all the weight on the wheels, ensuring the best braking is available. Meanwhile, the first officer advises the tower controller we have canceled our takeoff and will be clearing the runway, then returning to the terminal.

We turn back along the taxiway towards the ramp from where we just departed. After the first officer has switched the radio and checked in with the ground control air-traffic controller, he punches the number two radio transmit button to alert company maintenance that we're coming back. He asks for maintenance to come out to give number one engine a look-over. Then we go through the after-landing drill to re-secure the various systems.

So far all the engine parameters continue to be normal. "Should we shut it down?" the first officer asks. I confirm this is a good precaution, just to be on the safe side and limit any possible damage. But truthfully, at this point I suspect there's nothing wrong. I'm beginning to feel a little silly for having discontinued the takeoff. I'm thinking ahead to how long the maintenance check might take and if we'll need to top up our fuel load before departing again. We're the last flight to Houston tonight, so hopefully we won't cause any passengers to miss ongoing connections.

These are the thoughts going through my mind as we park the aircraft at the assigned gate and go through the normal shutdown checks. Then I get a call in my headset from a mechanic who has plugged into the aircraft's internal intercom system down on the ramp.

"Captain, you'll probably want to come out and see this."

I look quizzically at the first officer who heard him too. We bundle up in our winter coats and head down onto the tarmac. The mechanic and a few other interested ramp employees are gathered around the left side of the fuselage, peering into the left-hand engine, where the mechanic's flashlight is revealing something I've never seen before. I'm stunned.

The blades of the engine compressor are totally destroyed. These highly-engineered, critically-honed fan blades, as we call them, are responsible for drawing air into the engines. Successive stages of fan blades force the airstream further into a narrowing channel until the air is so compressed that its temperature has risen several degrees. At that point, it enters the combustion chamber, where fuel is sprayed in and the intense heat sets the mixture on fire. Without fan blades—there's no intake, no compression—no power! The blades on this left-hand engine are literally shredded—and not just the first layer. A cascade failure has shredded fan layers right down into the core of the engine. The first few stages are nothing more than broken, irregular shards of metal discs.

How did the engine keep running with so much damage? I'm astounded. And more to the point—I am wondering how this happened? The mechanic is reading my mind. He shifts his flashlight beam onto the left main tire. More shredded aircraft—this time rubber and chords from a blown tire. It's obvious now: the antiskid failure on the previous flight had also damaged our left-hand tires. Chunks of rubber had flown off as our speed and tire rpm increased. Some pieces must have scored a direct hit on the intake blades. Once the first blade shuddered and failed, the shards of metal and debris spread mayhem down the throat of the engine, completely destroying our multi-million-dollar thrust-producer in a matter of seconds.

Suddenly, I am very glad I chose to reject the takeoff. I am extremely grateful for the first officer's sharp eye and good judgment. He did not assume the gauge flicker was a slight irregularity not worth mentioning. Rather, he advised me in clear terms so I, as captain, would have the information to make the decision. Thankfully, this all happened at a low enough speed that the ***RTO (rejected takeoff)*** was easy and uneventful. For an RTO below 80 knots, there's not even any extra paperwork required—but I'll file a report anyway.

Later that night, while driving home, I began to play out the dangers we avoided tonight. If we'd had to stop from high speed on the slippery runway, or if we'd gotten airborne before the engine failed and had to fly to Ottawa on the remaining engine, we would have been much closer to the "danger zone" than anyone likes to go.

Thanks to the first officer's experience, we avoided those fates tonight. In hundreds or even thousands of previous flights, he had never seen the EPR needle flicker just like that. Like me, he may have seen it jitter quickly, in association with an engine backfire or stall. But never had he seen it drop so low, pause for a second, then bounce back. Neither had I. Why had that more conservative second opinion, arising in the back of my mind, ultimately take precedence? Why tonight?

A second opinion is often expressing itself within my mind. When is that "voice" a valid concern, and when is it merely the fearful chattering of an aging pilot becoming overly cautious? How to know? But tonight at least, I "earned the big bucks" by making the conservative choice and deciding not to go flying. Turns out, it was a good choice.

32

Squeezing Gas

✈ ✈ ✈

A320 Captain's Log: MBJ (Montego Bay, Jamaica)

According to an old aviation adage, the only time a pilot has too much fuel is when the plane is on fire. Pilots seldom grumble about having too much fuel.

Another aviation proverb claims there are three things most useless to a pilot: runway behind, altitude above and fuel left in the delivery truck. Pilots like fuel. Pilots *love* fuel. *Pilots are addicted to fuel.* We think about it constantly, from the time we start planning our flight until we are safely shut down at the destination. And then we're thinking about the fuel for the next flight.

We are parked on the ramp in Montego Bay, Jamaica on a typical, sweltering afternoon. The airport's official temperature is 34 degrees Celsius, but that's measured in a shaded box over the grass, somewhere on the airport infield. How much hotter is the air immediately over the black asphalt runway? Don't ask questions if you don't want the answers. But the fact is that hot air is thin air. Thin air produces poor aircraft performance, especially during takeoff.

This morning, we've just dropped off our inbound load of winter refugees. Now we're chock-a-block full with folks whose two-week all-inclusive is ending. They're a sunburned, tired and somewhat glum-looking bunch—they face returning to a Canadian winter.

We are expecting the usual challenges for our return flight to Toronto—scattered lines of thunderstorms along the coastal United States and typically unsettled weather in Southern Ontario. So we want fuel. Lots of fuel. Unhappily, the runway at **MBJ** (Sangster International Airport, Montego Bay, Jamaica) is only about 8000 feet long, which limits us. We have been working with our flight dispatcher and the load agents, trying to get the all-important numbers worked out regarding the weight of the fully loaded airplane. We are trying to squeeze every last drop of fuel into our tanks while respecting the maximum-allowed takeoff weight for this runway at today's temperature. Consequently, the fuel truck driver is hooked up to the refueling port until we receive our final information. Then, we squeeze in 10 more minutes' worth of fuel. It's not much, but it represents the flexibility to find a smoother route past thunderstorms, or one more turn around in a holding pattern before diverting to an alternate airport.

We push back on schedule. The instant we start the engines, we begin running out of fuel. From this point on, every event will be measured, not only by the clock but also the fuel gauges. Imagine an ever-shrinking circle around the aircraft, called our "radius of action." It represents how far we can fly before turning into a glider. Like liquid sand in a high-tech hourglass, the fuel relentlessly streams from the tanks, through the core of the CFM-56 engines, producing hot thrust, exhaust gases and noise–until that moment when the last drop is gone and then, with a deafening silence, the fires will go out. Engines will stop running. Unavoidable fact. It is a horrific moment-to-be-avoided, no matter what. No amount of denial or wishful thinking can make these facts go away.

As we taxi towards the button of the runway, I hope the extra 10 minutes of fuel won't be needed. I wish it was more because tonight this extra fuel could mean the difference between landing routinely at Toronto's Pearson International Airport or diverting to our alternate airport in Buffalo, New York.

I try not to think about that right now. The complications of a last minute, late-night, unscheduled landing at an airport in a different country—with all the extra issues of security and immigration—is something I hope to avoid. I read an incident report once about just such a diversion. One of the passengers had unresolved tax issues with Uncle Sam. He was flying happily home to Canada after a relaxing Cuban vacation, then surprisingly found himself diverted into Buffalo due to poor weather. The immigration agents, seeing his name on the passenger list, notified the tax authorities, who promptly sent officers to the flight to take the passenger into custody. Things can get unexpectedly complicated.

I don't imagine passengers concern themselves with fuel very much. They might briefly think, "I hope we have lots of fuel," if the pilot tells them a holding pattern is required due to landing delays. They may notice a fuel truck or two connected to the airplane when they first board. But that's about it. Hopefully, they never think about it again. But the pilots do—continuously. It surprises people when I explain some facts about fuel. For example, for economic reasons, we try to carry as little fuel as possible. "Don't you just 'fill 'er up?' like we do with our cars when we pull into a gas station?"

It's never that simple.

Fuel is one of the most significant operating expenses for an airline. Depending on market prices, a typical A320 runs through approximately $3000 of fuel per hour. A Jumbo A380, the largest passenger jet, runs through more than $25,000 of fuel per hour!

During a year's work, an airline pilot manages a multi-million-dollar fuel budget that can either make or break the airline's bottom line. Economies of scale for large airlines—with thousands of flights each year—means that even small fuel savings have a huge impact on the annual financial performance.

I've heard that some airlines tried using a bonus system for pilots who saved fuel but abandoned it because it went against aviation's culture of safety. No one wants to be the passenger on a flight with an overly aggressive captain who is trying to save fuel at the expense of safety. In fact, every pilot is highly motivated to fly as efficiently as possible and save fuel, because we all want our employers to survive financially in our cutthroat industry. So while we want to consume as little fuel as practicable, our safety parameters must never be compromised. This key balance between the safety culture and the economical operation of airlines is illustrated by a slogan from a poster, placed prominently in pilots' lounges and planning rooms: "If you think safety is expensive, try having an accident."

Fast-forward a few hours. It's almost midnight and we are on a long, gradual descent into Toronto, sliding across the Niagara Peninsula. In the daytime, we'd have a fantastic view of the falls. We have diverted a number of times since leaving Jamaica to avoid the worst of several lines of thunderstorms. Our fuel reserves are low, and just when I'm thinking things are going to work out, we switch our radio over to Toronto Arrival and hear flights ahead of us being issued holding clearances. The level of tension on the flight deck ramps up a notch. The first officer and I both take a furtive glance at our fuel gauges.

An Air France Airbus A330 has misjudged the exit taxiway and is now stuck halfway off the landing runway. One set of its huge wheels is mired up to the axels in the soft grass. This runway is now closed for an indefinite time. No one knows if the closure will last half-an-hour or half the night. Suddenly, long streams of airliners, flowing into this busy airport from all directions, are circling into assigned holding patterns.

Our holding clearance comes next. The harried controller transmits the details—the first officer writes them down and reads them back to ensure all is correct. He then begins tapping the necessary buttons on the data-entry keypad, converting these instructions into the mysterious language of our flight guidance computer system. He works as rapidly as possible because we are closing in on our first turn. If he enters the data too fast, the computer refuses to respond for a few agonizing seconds.

I am reminded that our state-of-the-art electronics are just as prone to the same foibles as all other computers. Processors need time to work. Sometimes keystrokes don't register properly because the computer is busy doing something else. The first officer may push the same key again, trying to get a response. But sometimes the first stroke did register in the keypad's buffer, so the extra keystrokes cause an error in the required syntax. He must erase the message and start again. All this goes on as we are rushing headlong towards our required turning point at five miles per minute.

I've been on "the Bus" long enough to know about these limitations, so without hesitation, I convert the aircraft into a less-automated flight mode. By monitoring the raw data displayed on our navigation instruments, I begin the first turn into our assigned hold, dialing a new heading into the auto-pilot control panel.

As we roll out of the turn into the assigned holding pattern, the first officer finishes typing and within a few seconds the little troll who resides somewhere within the black boxes deep in the belly of the airplane accomplishes its calculations and draws green lines on the screen, showing where it figures our hold should be. Both pilots check the indicated flight path and when we're happy that it's exactly what we want, I push the button authorizing Otto (auto-pilot) to follow that line. At the same time, I manually select the airspeed, slowing us down to reduce fuel consumption. Our goal now is to extend the time we can stay in our holding pattern by burning the least amount of fuel possible.

Meanwhile, we are busily communicating our situation. Our flight dispatcher must be updated and reminded of our fuel predicament. If a diversion to Buffalo becomes necessary, we will arrive there suddenly and many other people will need to be alerted. We also provide our local Toronto airport agent with an updated "guestimate" of our arrival time. He'll have gates and ground crews to reschedule. According to our currently-assigned hold time, and the abacus-wielding troll lurking inside the black boxes, we are close to the edge. We will soon be diverting to Buffalo unless landings in Toronto resume quickly.

We have one more trick up our sleeves to help avoid diverting to Buffalo. The airport at Niagara Falls (Airport Code: **IAG**) is closer than Buffalo, almost beneath us at times. If the weather there meets requirements, and if the approach and landing facilities are operational, we can use **IAG** as our alternate airport instead of **BUF**. The resulting fuel savings might extend our holding time a few critical minutes. We use this tactic frequently. It is called "shortening up the alternate."

It's a calculated risk. If the strategy fails, our night's work will become even more difficult because the offices at Niagara probably aren't fully staffed late at night. If we land there, we'll face increased delays—refueling, customs, immigration and security clearances—before returning to Toronto.

On the other hand, an unexpected diversion to Buffalo also throws a slightly smaller wrench into the works. It is a bigger, busier airport, but chances are we won't be the only flight diverting there. Delays will occur there too if the demands on available personnel are suddenly exceeded.

After a short discussion with the first officer and flight dispatch, we all agree "shortening up" is a reasonable risk tonight. Airline flying is always about risk management. These risks tonight are not safety related, but rather, related to customer service and financial concerns. Whether shortening up will turn out to be a good choice depends on how quickly the airport crews get that giant Airbus A330 clear of the runway in Toronto.

During these ongoing communications, the first officer and I have

been working busily, confirming the weather and landing facilities at
IAG are operational, and previewing the approach procedures. It's
daunting and disorienting to suddenly begin a nighttime approach into
an unfamiliar airport. Neither of us has been there before. We don't
want to go there now. But if it's required, we will have only about 15
minutes between the decision to divert and our touch down. Descending
rapidly towards an unfamiliar airport in the dark is not the time to be
heads-down in the books, studying the details of the airport. As much
as possible, we try to prepare ahead of time.

I ask our dispatcher to phone Niagara to confirm that our contracted
service company is working this time of night and to alert them that
we might be dropping in. It's not a prospect I relish at the end of a
long day's work. Since early this morning, when we originally left
Toronto, we've dealt with a wintry departure with complex calculations
to account for slippery airport surfaces. We've been through a rigorous
de-icing process, ensuring the wings were properly sprayed before
takeoff. Then, we spent the next several hours dodging thunderstorms
and dealing with the vagaries of Cuban ATC, working our way down
to Jamaica. On the ground in Montego Bay, we literally sweated over
the calculations for another complicated departure, followed by a maximum performance takeoff, then another round of thunderstorm pinball
all the way back to Toronto. The day has been a continual headlong
rush from one destination to another—re-calculating, re-planning, re-
adapting—then doing it over again. The long hours begin to take a toll
on our mental sharpness.

If we do land at Niagara, we'll have more fine-pencil calculating to
do. The flight crew and attendants will need to check our duty time. A
diversion to any alternate airport might be our last permitted flight of
the day. Either or both of the crews might face a legally-required
rest period before pushing on to Toronto. Diversions can become
complicated.

We've been scrambling since Toronto Center issued our surprise
holding clearance. Along with the fuel-related issues, we also need to
keep the flight attendants and passengers informed. I call the purser
on the intercom to give him a summary of the situation and to check if
our passengers are asleep or awake. In other words, should I make an
announcement? "They're all pretty much awake, getting ready for the

landing," he tells me. I hand control of the aircraft to the first officer so I can give the folks a quick briefing, mentioning the delays into Toronto. I leave out any hints that we might end up landing somewhere else. At this point, there's no sense worrying them with rumors and possibilities—especially if anyone has ongoing issues with Uncle Sam and the IRS.

For the next few minutes, we carve our way around our racetrack pattern south of Toronto, along with several other planes at different altitudes. Only ATC knows how many aircraft in total are approaching from all directions.

The closing of a major runway has caused a tidal wave, rippling back through the sea of late-night inbound traffic. Our fuel reserves have been steadily counting down towards zero. Now we're down to those last 10 minutes of extra fuel we put on at Montego Bay. We have just one more lap around the racetrack. We turn outbound. Then we'll be down to our minimum safe fuel to reach Niagara Falls. I let ATC and our flight dispatcher both know we either need to begin an approach into Toronto or divert to Niagara.

My ears perk up as I hear ATC start calling flights from the bottom of our holding stack, sending them along the path to Toronto. The runway is clear. The backlog of landing flights is flowing again—slowly.

That's a hopeful sign, but knowing there are several flights below and ahead of us in the stack, I am resigned to making my inaugural landing at Niagara Falls International airport.

Then, our dispatcher says something wonderful. "Standby," she tells us. "We have another company flight ahead of you with larger fuel reserves. I'm phoning Toronto Approach to request they give you priority ahead of the Miami flight."

A last-minute reprieve? Is this possible? On the radio tuned to the air traffic frequency, we overhear ATC giving our company's Miami flight a clearance to leave the holding pattern. I fear our dispatcher's deliverance plan has come too late. I wish I could jump on the frequency and negotiate a priority arrival myself, but this would be a breach of protocol. No one but the air traffic controllers have the authority to decide the arrival sequence of inbound traffic, and they do this according to industry-prescribed standards—unless someone should declare an emergency. Going to an alternate landing site may be inconvenient, but it does not qualify as an emergency.

The call to our Miami inbound flight is followed almost immediately by another call, rescinding their clearance. "Your dispatch department wants the Montego Bay flight in ahead of you." He re-issues them another hold, then calls us with the clearance we've been anxiously waiting for. He assigns us a new pathway to fly clear of the flights below, then gives us a clearance to descend into the routing for the final approach to Toronto.

Quickly, and with a sense of relief, we put away the standby charts and information that we've been dragging out for Niagara, and reinstate our normal approach to Toronto's main runway. We can still break off for an emergency diversion if something else bad happens along the way—but it doesn't. The weather remains good. No one else slides off the runways or taxiways. We touch down and taxi in, arriving at our gate only a few minutes behind schedule.

As far as our passengers are aware, besides a boring half-hour circling the skies over southern Ontario, it's been a routine flight. Many of them probably figure that during this dull passage of time in the cabin, we pilots have been grabbing a short nap, while Otto and ATC have been flying the plane.

After I've smiled gratefully and said goodbye to all the good people who ultimately pay my salary, I return to my seat to process the final shutdown checklists with the first officer. We tuck the plane in for the night and stuff our personal gear back into our flight bags, thankful to be finished.

Just before switching off the electrical power and plunging the cockpit into darkness, I pick up the microphone and call the flight dispatcher. I want her to know what a good job she did and how much I appreciated it. She came up with a plan to save us all, and especially our passengers, from a huge inconvenience. She also saved our company extra costs on landing fees and expenses related to customs, immigration and security—not to mention passenger loss of goodwill. Tonight, she has earned the big bucks and deserves the credit. Sometimes, someone does see the big picture and acts on it.

33

Boring is Good—Trust Me

✈ ✈ ✈

"Don't you get bored?" The question is posed by our visitor to the flight deck—an agreeable, middle-aged gentleman.

Pre-911, we could invite guests to the flight deck. This was a great way to meet some of our passengers. A visit to the business end of the jet often helped calm nervous flyers.

The most common questions people asked were about the plane, where we were, or how fast and high were we flying. Every now and then someone asked, "Aren't you bored?" I guess the implication was, "Everyone knows the computers fly the plane. So don't you get bored, sitting there drinking coffee, just looking out the window?"

I began to turn this question over in my mind, looking for the best answer.

I'm sitting at the controls of a multi-million-dollar vehicle—a wonder of human engineering and precision technology. An airliner is one of the most advanced pieces of machinery our civilization has ever developed, reflecting our understanding and relative mastery of aerodynamics, materials and construction, electronics, computer technology, power-plant engineering and navigation. I have all the controls of this marvelous vehicle within easy reach. At the turn of a button or pressure on the "joystick," I can change its flight path in any direction, including vertically. If I did this carelessly, I could easily injure or even kill our carbon-based occupants. I am acutely aware of my responsibility for the safety of everyone on board.

I am also constantly aware of the inner workings of the amazing machinery enveloping us, protecting us from the outside environment, making it possible for us to travel and stay alive. The engines are constructed from the most advanced metallurgy known, spinning at thousands of revolutions per minute, operating under tremendous extremes of pressure and temperature. The fuel system is keeping the fires burning and the lights on. The air conditioning and pressurization systems are maintaining a livable, breathable atmosphere inside the plane. I hear the constant background noises and my ears tell me all is well, even without looking at the myriad instrument panels and indicators. All our systems are "Go." If this changes, I am primed to quickly launch into any required checklists and procedures to prevent a catastrophe.

We are surrounded by dozens, if not hundreds of other flights. I am listening carefully in my headset for any directives issues by ATC, to keep us safely separated from other planes.

It must be relatively calm today or we would not be accepting visits to the flight deck. But it could easily be otherwise. The surrounding sea of air could be rough, keeping us busy, seeking smooth altitudes. The rivers of air flowing around us—called jet streams—can become turbulent without warning, injuring the fragile occupants of this metal tube. We are often busy avoiding dangerous thunderstorms. There are valid reasons we ask our passengers to keep their seat belts fastened as much as practicable.

We are visitors in a potentially hazardous environment, hurtling across the top of the atmosphere. At 35,000 feet, approximately 75% of the earth's thin atmosphere is below us. At this altitude, the partial pressure of oxygen is so low, were the cabin to suddenly depressurize, our time of useful consciousness is measured in seconds, not minutes. If the lack of oxygen didn't kill us, the –50 degree temperature surely would. Our drill to deal with a dozen such emergencies is continually sitting on the edge of my memory, ready to recall and instantly enact if needed.

Our speed through this rarefied atmosphere is 78% of the speed of sound, which at this moment means over 500 miles per hour. That's about three times more violent than any hurricane ever recorded. If somehow the power of this blast got under a piece of our fuselage, the force would rip the aircraft apart. Although an airliner is incredibly strong for the stresses it encounters, it is actually insubstantial. It is akin to a wire frame, sheathed in tinfoil—or more recently, carbon-fiber cloth.

Beyond the technological marvels that sustain us here, I'm constantly in awe of the world around. With the naked eye, I can see into the depths of the planets and stars above, light years into our discernible universe. At this altitude, my circle of view on the earth's surface extends over a hundred miles in all directions. I see our planet as no one in all human history ever saw until a very few decades ago. Even today, when airline flying is so common, most humans on our planet have never flown and never will. Yet I routinely study the lay of million-year-old geologic formations, the flow of ancient river valleys or fantastic plains and canyons formed over eons. I see the evidence of human civilizations, hugging the rivers and shorelines of lakes and oceans. I see the vast, barren wildernesses that remain relatively unsullied by human civilization. I constantly wonder about our place as fragile creatures in an incomprehensible world.

Beyond our machinery and this spectacular front row view of the universe, we are immersed in the dynamics of our constant, headlong motion. We are rushing towards our destination—and our destiny. Our intent is to find a very small patch of pavement, thousands of miles away, and return to earth there. Any other outcome would be disastrous. We can only return safely to earth through an extremely careful, painstaking diminution of the energy currently stored within our aircraft and our very bodies. Our potential and kinetic energy, in the form of altitude and speed—injected into us during the takeoff, acceleration and climb to altitude—must be carefully managed and dissipated, or we will not survive the landing.

To this end, I am monitoring our position and progress at all times. My co-pilot and I are continually keeping an eye on what's ahead and how we will get there. We watch our machinery and technology. We watch the weather. We watch our fuel. We especially watch our fuel. We only have a fixed amount. If any unplanned changes occur, we need to detect these as soon as possible, while we still have options, such as diverting to an alternate airport. Above all else, we must never, never, never run out of fuel.

All this flashes through my mind as I try to muster up an answer to the question, "Aren't you bored?" But I realize there is no way to communicate all this. I merely shrug and smile my most reassuring smile and say, "Boring is good. Trust me, you wouldn't like 'exciting.'"

34

JAX is Not My Home

✈   ✈   ✈

Captain's Log:
2002 / A320 / Cruise over northern Florida

The flight deck feels dim and disjointed as I sit bathed in the soft glow of instrument displays, punctuated occasionally by intense flashes of distant lightning. The first officer sits to my right. The eerie light gives her gleaming white uniform shirt a spectral quality. She hunches over her radar screen, right arm propped up on the dash panel, left arm reaching towards the center console, where she deftly tweaks the controls, coaxing out a clearer message. Analyzing weather radar can sometimes feel like the electronic version of scanning chicken innards for omens.

I too should be consulting these flaring and fading oracles of colored electrons, phosphorescing in that picture. And I will. But not now. I'm tired and the day's already been too long. For now, I am content to gaze left out my side window, mesmerized. We're tracking along the Atlantic shore of northern Florida, heading home from Miami to Montreal. Tonight, the entire length of the sunshine state is billowing with thunderstorms. Two hundred miles ahead, the coastline of the Carolinas sweeps eastward, dragging a flashing curtain of storms across our path.

I gaze through my reflection in the night-darkened glass panel. Lightning erupts in the swelling tops of a nearby storm, towering 20,000 feet above us. We're at 35,000 feet and I smile inwardly, recalling how prognosticators back in the 1950s believed that by now, jetliners would be routinely cruising well above all the weather. Naive. How could the meteorologists of the day not have known the full height of these storms? World War II aircraft had already flown up to the edges of our sky, exploring the phenomenon of the jet stream and other mysteries. But perhaps they hadn't explored these heights regularly enough to understand. Weather radar was just being developed and was not yet available to pilots.

Then something catches my eye through a break in the undercast. It appears as a serene dark pool in the midst of a noisy swarm of city lights. I begin to see it's an airport almost below us. Within that darkness, tiny festive patterns of amber, green and blue lights outline runways, taxiways and ramps. A white beacon strobes briefly from the center. It feels like a mirage. A false invitation to rest and a warm bed and an end to the journey.

I recall the story of a senior colleague, who one night over the prairies of Saskatchewan, found himself hopelessly surrounded by two closing lines of thunderstorms. With too little altitude, too little fuel and too much weather, he wisely chose to divert into the nearest airport he could find. The runway at Swift Current was barely long enough and the airport had no handling services for a DC-9. Yet everyone lived to tell the tale. A quick glance at my navigation display shows the magenta code **JAX**, revealing that the airport beckoning from below is Jacksonville, and I briefly picture us circling down into that peaceful pool, to find safe harbor.

But **JAX** is not my home. It is not our destination. As much as I might long to avoid the strain and perhaps even fear that lies ahead tonight as we dare to challenge 50,000-foot Goliaths of turbulence, hail and lightning, I know that that's exactly what we intend to do. That's what we do for our living. It's why we earn "the big bucks."

I'm confident, from previous trips up and down this route, that the aircraft, crew and fuel load will be up to the task—like so many pebbles in a slingshot, ready to slay giants. Once more, we will safely cross over sea and foreign soil to regain the comforts of home—my own bed, my house on the outskirts of Montreal, my family. That's where all that is dear to me resides. And I won't be satisfied with any other diversion or destination. No matter how much the respite might be welcomed, it would only be temporary. That unrequited longing would still compel. When home beckons on the horizon, nothing else will suffice. This urgency has even been named in the vocabulary of aviation accident investigators. It's called "get-home-itis." It is characterized by the pilot making poor choices and pressing on, despite dangerously deteriorating conditions.

Maybe that's the cautionary thought that snaps me out of my reverie. I return my attention to inside the shadowy flight deck and join the first officer in scanning ghostly radar images. By painstakingly coordinating them with the distant flashes we see through the front window, we begin to plot our way between the hazardous, roiling clouds that separate us from our destination.

Home.

35

Final Flight

✈   ✈   ✈

"Captain, you put in your name for the early retirement program. Are you sure you want to retire?"

The phone rang one pleasant autumn morning as I was enjoying my morning coffee and planning my day. This question momentarily caught me off guard and I paused, my mind racing. Our airline was going through a bankruptcy. These stresses, added to the ultra-security measures added since the 9-11 disaster, had significantly changed many aspects of the career I loved. I had been wondering for several years now how much longer I wanted to keep at this. Many thoughts raced through my mind as I formulated my answer.

So I stood there, rapidly reviewing my feelings about retirement. This was not a new issue for me. Five years earlier, I was gathered with some colleagues in the Chief Pilot's office to commemorate the twenty-year milestone of our careers. We were lined up against a wall for a group photo. As I stood there, looking all captainly in my uniform, I had one of those rare moments in my life when an idea arose clearly inside my mind. It said: "This part of your life is over now. You've achieved what you wanted. It's time to move on."

Time to move on? To what? Where? That was unclear. I only knew that some part of me was finished with airline flying. I had accomplished my dream. I had flown successfully for several years as an airline captain. I had flown a significant number of hours, through all the usual dangers and challenges the job entailed, and that was all well and good. But still, this was not the end-all and be-all of a human life. Something always lay ahead. Sometimes the heart knows before the mind when it's time to move on.

So, for five years I'd been looking and wondering how to wind this all up. All the while, I was working and wondering about how I could afford to retire early. All the usual questions played on my mind.

What next? Why? Where's the purpose in a human life? What's the purpose of my life?

Then our company offered these opportunities for an early retirement with some added incentives. I listened intently to the reasons some of my colleagues expressed as they pondered applying for this same option. "I can't afford to retire." "I'm paying too much alimony." "I have too large a mortgage."

It surprised me that these accomplished, professional people, at this advanced stage of their careers, could have so little financial solvency—or so they claimed. I examined my own life to see what arguments existed to prevent me from retiring. One day, while talking to a friend about all this, he chuckled over my concerns about the early retirement penalties that would reduce my pension and said, "Ah yes. The golden handcuffs we make for ourselves."

The "golden handcuffs"—handcuffs of my own creation! I realized then it was my own expectations, fears and longings for comfort that held me back. I did a little more soul-searching, and instead of looking at the penalties that would apply to my finances if I retired early, I began to ask, "How much do I really need?" What would be sufficient to keep me and my family solvent through the foreseeable years of retirement, keeping in mind the vagaries of the economic realities and uncertainties of life? I calculated it several times, looked at various angles, and decided on a number. Then it became clear—I had enough. So, what then was holding me back?

"When my notice of retirement crosses the Chief Pilot's desk, I want him to say, 'Who's that? Does he work for us?'"

This was the humorous way that pilots sometimes described their goal to achieve a career free of any major incidents and accidents, and most of all, unhappy appearances on the Six O'clock News. They hoped their Chief Pilot would never have to deal with issues they'd inadvertently created. We all hoped to retire with a clean record.

The biggest nightmare for most pilots was that we would end up the target of an official accident investigation. We'd seen the unfair criticisms that so often arose from such events—usually from people with no understanding of the flight deck environment. It never seemed justified that these armchair experts, afforded almost unlimited time and resources, should so minutely dissect the pilot's decisions. Critiques from outsiders about a pilot's actions never seemed to adequately account for the way these decisions are made, by necessity, "in the heat of battle," under the unrelenting, dynamic pressures of a vehicle that can never just stop and must be continually controlled. These decisions are formed at critical moments, based upon inadequate data, and often outdated, faulty information—decisions forced upon us within seconds. This contrasted drastically with post-crash investigations, where each decision was thrashed, analyzed and simulated, and then criticized by people whose jobs were completely foreign to a flight deck. Post-crash investigators might as well be commenting on life on another planet.

Worst of all, these judges had no concept of working in such a dynamic environment, where the threat of an accident constantly looms, and might suddenly erupt so fast as to catch you completely unaware. One captain used to point out how, by comparison, "The biggest danger these experts faced in a day's work is accidentally running over their own fingers with the wheels of their own chairs as they fumble for a pencil they just dropped." That's probably an exaggeration. It does express the frustration that pilots often feel regarding investigations.

So it was that pilots, after amassing an accident-free record and nearing the end of their career, become more and more concerned that they don't mess up. We'd all heard of one captain or another, who after dozens of years, hundreds of flights and literally thousands of accident-free hours, had dinged a wing tip on his last flight, causing thousands of dollars' worth of injury to his aircraft and leaving a dark spot on an otherwise perfect safety record. None of us wanted to be that guy.

I thought back to the night when I finally submitted my application for the early retirement offer. The airport was quiet as we pulled into the arrival gate after the last flight of the day—the late arrival from Miami. I made my way upstairs to the locker room where I changed out of my uniform jacket and stowed my flight bag. Just before leaving the now deserted flight-planning room, I took the retirement application out of my inside pocket, where I had been carrying it for several days, unfolded it and looked at it again. I made sure I had checked the appropriate boxes for the options available. I hesitated for an instant, then refolded the form and popped it through the slot into the company mailbox. Done. Now, to wait and see what happens next. "Probably the deal won't even get down to my seniority," I told myself.

Now, a couple weeks later and here I was, the company representative waiting on the other end of the line for my response. "Do you still want to accept the early retirement package?"

"Yes, I do."

"Okay, we'll begin processing you immediately. I see you're flying another Miami trip tomorrow. That will be your last flight. Thank you." She hung up. I stood there for a moment, my head spinning slowly. That was it? I walked back to the kitchen table and sat down.

"Who was that?" my wife asked.

"The company. Apparently, I'm retired—almost."

"Good," she said.

When pilots retire, there is often some special fuss made about their last flight. Sometimes the home airport fire department will set up a cascade of water from the emergency vehicles that the aircraft taxis through after that last landing. Sometimes a small celebratory group will meet the captain as he or she walks off their aircraft for the last time. I was grateful nothing like this occurred. I don't enjoy being the center of attention.

When I mentioned the fact of my last flight to my first officer the next day, he must have communicated this to the flight attendants. During our stopover in Miami, when the co-pilot and I returned from preparing our return flight plan, we arrived back at the aircraft to find a "farewell party" had been hurriedly staged in the Airbus galley, complete with a small cake from an airport deli. Our crew shared a few moments of celebratory cake and coffee just before our homeward-bound passengers began boarding.

A few hours later, as we descended into Montreal's terminal airspace and switched our radio to their frequency, the familiar voice of the arrival controller offered a short, congratulatory message. Evidently my Chief Pilot had figured out, in the nick of time, that I did indeed work here, and arranged this short goodbye announcement with our ATC colleagues. The Chief Pilot also met me outside the customs arrival doors. He greeted me with a warm handshake, then led me upstairs to his office where he presented an official retirement memento—a portrait of an Airbus A319, in flight over a sea of clouds.

I was happy there were very few observers around for all this. Again, it was the last late flight of the night, and the terminal building was almost empty. I accepted his warm thanks, smiling inwardly. This gentleman had only recently been promoted to his new role as base manager. A few short years earlier, I had been his ground school instructor at the beginning of his new career. Later, he had flown briefly as my first officer. Now he had worked his way up to captain on our new regional jets—the very ones for which I'd helped develop the pilot training courses. Now he was my boss, sending me off into my "golden years." Life draws these funny circles of coincidences, doesn't it?

I thanked him for his genuine warmth. Then I made my way out one last time, walking through the empty flight planning center, across the now-quiet terminal building, to the far reaches of the employee parking lot. This part of my life was over. There would still be an official retirement "bash" at a local pub, staged by our pilots' union. At the end of the year, there was an annual company and union-sponsored retirement gala for all that year's retirees. Then, it truly was finished.

In the end, what was this journey all about? I accomplished my goal to become an airline captain, but then I felt compelled to move on—to what? What was the point? Was all the financial investment, constant effort, strains and stresses, irregular working schedules with missed home events, such as birthdays and special family days, worth the effort? After all my struggles to obtain and keep my career, why did I voluntarily leave early? Why did I choose to become a permanent member of Mr. McPlane's two-out-of-three statistic that I first learned about during his welcoming speech so many years ago? I had no easy answer—only a sense that it was time. I'm not good at repeating the same things over and over. I just felt a sense that it was time to move on and spend the rest of my years seeking new adventures. It was time to retire and leave my chair to the younger pilots. It was time to give way to the next generation.

Life itself is ultimately a one-way passage. Moving on, whether voluntarily or involuntarily, is an unavoidable part of the journey. We might as well try to grow and absorb something along the way that increases our storehouse of experience. If we can enjoy the trip along the way, accepting faithfully whatever comes next, then maybe that's the best we can do. It seems we have little choice in this.

But what of all the people who invested time and energy into my life? This drives home for me the fact that there is no such thing as a "self-made" person. We are all deeply dependent upon those who went before us and we owe a debt of gratitude to them—and which we're obliged to pass on to those who come after us. Our role is to continually support, care for and *uplift* one another, in the belief that ultimately, we are all on the same journey. A journey from what we are to something we will become—something beyond our power to comprehend.

The journey continues.

Appendixes

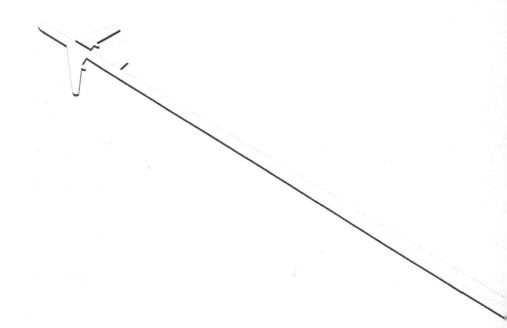

Uplift

✈   ✈   ✈

Uplift is happening all around us, one way and another. Maybe that's significant. Here are some definitions and perspectives on "uplift."

1. **Uplift** (transitive verb)
    a. to lift up: elevate; to cause something (e.g. a portion of the earth's surface) to rise above adjacent areas.
    b. to improve spiritual, social or intellectual conditions.

2. **Uplift** (in Aviation):
    a. (verb) The action of transferring fuel from a truck or hydrant into an aircraft. "Will we be uplifting fuel at this stop?"
    b. (noun) "What's our uplift?" (i.e. "How much fuel was added to the tanks?"
    c. (noun) The lifting of air by surface features.
    d. (adjective) "We need our fuel uplift information."

3. In science fiction, **uplift** is a developmental process to transform a certain species of animals into more intelligent beings by other, already-intelligent beings. This is usually accomplished by cultural, technological, or evolutionary interventions like genetic engineering but any fictional or real process can be used. The earliest appearance of the concept is in H.G. Wells' 1896 novel, *The Island of Doctor Moreau* and more recently appears in David Brin's *Uplift* series and other science fiction works.

4. **Uplift,** in my own imaginings about the world: Perhaps the entire human race is on a trajectory from what we were to what we are becoming. Perhaps, individually and collectively, whether by the grace of a supreme creator or the processes of natural evolution, if you prefer, our struggles in the dirt, our daily lives, this entire earthly experience, is an *uplift* toward something beyond our imaginations.

Further Reading, Viewing

✈ ✈ ✈

Books:

Fate is the Hunter: A Pilot's Memoir by Ernest K. Gann. This is my all-time classic aviation book. Gann puts us right into the flight deck beside him as he survives many adventures in the early days of the airline industry.

Skyfaring: A Journey with a Pilot by Mark Vanhoenacker. A beautifully written ode to the poetry of flight in the 21st century.

Cockpit Confidential: Everything You Need to Know About Air Travel: Questions, Answers, and Reflections by Patrick Smith. Some interesting and sometimes hard-hitting information and opinions about the airline industry from an experienced pilot who knows his stuff.

From the Flight Deck: Plane Talk and Sky Science by Doug Morris. An informative look at the airline travel industry. Morris answers a lot of questions that passengers often ask—or should.

Night Flight by Antoine de Saint-Exupery. One of the all-time classics that reminds us of how tough the flying game was a few decades ago.

A Gift of Wings by Richard Bach. Superb short articles from an always-entertaining author.

One Day at Kitty Hawk: The Untold Story of the Wright Brothers and the Airplane by John Evangelist Walsh. The most informative and easy-to-read account of the inventors of our modern airplane.

Movies:

Sully, starring Tom Hanks, directed by Clint Eastwood. One of the few movies I've ever seen where the flying sequences seemed realistic. Highly recommended.

TV Series:

Mayday, also known as *Air Crash Investigation* in Australia, South Africa, United Kingdom, Asia and some European countries, and *Air Emergency and Air Disasters* in the United States (both ended in

2008), is a Canadian documentary television program investigating air crashes, near-crashes, hijackings, bombings and other disasters.

Mayday uses re-enactments and computer-generated imagery to reconstruct for its audiences the sequence of events leading up to each disaster. In addition, aviation experts, retired pilots and crash investigators are interviewed explaining how these emergencies came about, how they were investigated and how they could have been prevented.

The Co-pilot

I am the co-pilot. I sit on the right.
It's up to me to be quick and bright;
I never talk back for I have regrets,
But I have to remember what the Captain forgets.

I make out the Flight Plan and study the weather,
Pull up the gear, stand by to feather;
Make out the mail forms and do the reporting,
And fly the old crate while the Captain is courting.

I take the readings, adjust the power,
Put on the heaters when we're in a shower;
Tell him where we are on the darkest night,
And do all the bookwork without any light.

I call for my Captain and buy him cokes;
I always laugh at his corny jokes,
And once in awhile when his landings are rusty
I always come through with, "By gosh it's gusty!"

All in all I'm a general stooge,
As I sit on the right of the man I call "Scrooge";
I guess you think that is past understanding,
But maybe some day he will give me a landing.

—Keith Murray

The Rules of Flying

✈ ✈ ✈

• Takeoff is optional. Landing is mandatory.

• Flying isn't dangerous. Crashing is what's dangerous.

• It's always better to be down here wishing you were up there than up there wishing you were down here.

• The ONLY time you have too much fuel is when you're on fire.

• The propeller is a big fan in front of the plane which cools the pilots. When it stops, watch them sweat.

• A "good" landing is any landing you walk away from. A "great" landing is one where you can use the airplane again.

• Learn from the mistakes of others. You won't live long enough to make them all yourself.

• The probability of survival is inversely proportional to the angle of arrival.

• Never let an aircraft take you somewhere your brain didn't get to five minutes earlier.

• Stay out of clouds. The silver lining everyone keeps talking about might be another airplane going in the opposite direction.

• There are three simple rules for making a smooth landing. Unfortunately, no one knows what they are.

• You start your flying career with a full bag of luck and an empty bag of experience. The trick is to fill the bag of experience before you empty the bag of luck.

• If all you can see out of the window is the ground going round and round, and all you can hear is a loud commotion from the passengers, things are not as they should be.

Glossary

✈ ✈ ✈

Airport Identifiers—Three (IATA) letter abbreviations used to identify the airports in this book:

USA:
BOS—Boston Logan
BUF—Buffalo
HOU—Houston
IAG—Niagara Falls International
LAS—Las Vegas
LAX—Los Angeles
LGA—LaGuardia
JAX—Jacksonville
MIA—Miami
ORD—Chicago O'Hare
SFO—San Francisco

Canada:
YEG—Edmonton
YHZ—Halifax
YQI—Yarmouth
YQR—Regina
YQT—Thunder Bay
YSB—Sudbury
YUL—Montreal
YVR—Vancouver
YWG—Winnipeg
YXE—Saskatoon
YYC—Calgary
YYZ—Toronto

Jamaica:
MBJ or MKJS—Montego Bay

ADF radios (Automatic Direction Finder) – A navigation radio that points toward specific beacons located at known sites.

After start / landing sequence – A specific checklist or memorized drill carried out to reconfigure and/or confirm the condition of the aircraft systems.

Airport porter – Provides curb check-in and helps passengers with luggage, wheel chairs, etc.

Airstarter – A ground-based source of compressed air used to start jet engines when an onboard **APU** source is not available.

APU (Auxiliary Power Unit) – A small turbine in the tail or belly of the aircraft. It provides electricity and compressed air for cabin temperature control and for starting our engines.

ATC (Air Traffic Control/Controllers) – Provides navigation and traffic flow prioritizing services to all aircraft.

ATIS, ATS (Automatic Terminal Information Service) – A recorded broadcast of the weather observations at a particular airport.

ATPL (Airline Transport Pilot License) – The highest level of commercial pilot licensing.

Base [Flight Operations] Director – The supervisory pilot responsible for administration duties at a particular pilot base.

Bleed Air – Air taken from the compressor sections of jet engines used to provide air conditioning and pressurization for the interior cabin of the aircraft.

Briefings – Information meetings of personnel before training sessions or flights.

Captain – The pilot-in-command.

CBUs / Carbon Based Units – Tongue-in-cheek expression for human beings. See SBUs.

CAVU – Ceiling and Visibility Unlimited. Shorthand code for excellent weather.

Checklists – All important aircraft operating procedures are accomplished using checklists.

Check rides – The many ways our operational competency and knowledge is tested, either in a flight simulator or on the actual aircraft, by supervisory pilots called "check pilots."

Chief Pilot – Supervisory pilot responsible for administering the technical operations of a particular type of aircraft.

Circuit / Pattern – The rectangular path an aircraft will follow from a takeoff and back around to an immediate landing.

Coffin Corner – The top corner on an airliner's high altitude performance envelope where the maximum design speed and lowest design speed (stall speed) coincide.

Compressor Stalls – Disruptions of the flow of air into the compressor (the forward section of a jet engine) usually producing a loud thumping noise—like an engine backfire.

CBT – Computer-Based Training.

Compressors, N1, N2, Spools, Turbines – Jet engines are comprised of (usually) two sets of compressors and turbines.

Cross-bleed Start – Using the compressed (bleed) air from an engine that is running to start another engine.

Crew members – Flight decks are crewed by at least two pilots, the **captain** and **first officer**. Some older aircraft required a third crewmember, a **second officer** or flight engineer.

CYA – "Cover your ass."

Deadhead – Transferring a pilot as a passenger to operate or return from a flight.

De-crabbing – Final adjustments of the aircraft heading with the runway.

EKG – Electrocardiogram.

Electronic Glide Slope – Part of the ILS that provides vertical guidance for aircraft during approach and landing.

EPR – Engine Pressure Ratio. A primary power-setting instrument for jet engines.

ETA – Estimated Time of Arrival.

FAF (Final Approach Fix) – checkpoint where pilots will complete configuring the aircraft for landing, ensuring the wing flaps and landing gear are properly set. Typically, four miles from the runway.

Final Approach Track – The line extending into the centerline of the landing runway.

Final Flap Setting – The amount that wing flaps will be extended for the rest of the approach and landing.

First Officer (FO or co-pilot) – Second-in-command on the aircraft.

Flight Attendant – The crew member charged with exercising the captain's responsibility for the safety of passengers. They may also provide en route service amenities.

Flight Deck – The pilots' cockpit.

Flight Instructor / Instructor's Rating – Once pilots obtain a commercial license, allowing them to work for hire, a further course qualifies them, rating them as a flight instructor.

FFS – Full Flight Simulator. A full sized, fully functional mockup of an aircraft flight deck.

Fleet Canucks – Classic Canadian two-seat light aircraft.

Flight Engineer – A maintenance-oriented flight-crew member. Think "Scotty" on Star Trek.

Flight Levels – Above a defined altitude (18,000 in NA), pilots set their altimeters to a common reference point so they fly at the same altitudes relative to other aircraft.

Flying circuits – See Circuits

FO – First Officer.

Flight Operations Director – The supervisory pilot responsible for administering an airline's entire flight department.

Galley – Onboard kitchen or food preparation area.

Go Around – Balked landing, missed approach—breaking off a landing and climbing back up to a maneuvering altitude.

GPU – Ground Power Unit – a power source that connects to supply a parked aircraft with electrical power during ground operations.

GPWS – Ground Proximity Warning System.

High-speed Buffet – When the maximum speed is exceeded for a jet aircraft's wing design, aerodynamic shock waves may arise that produce a vibration, or buffeting, in the airframe.

Honey-wagons – Euphemism for the lavatory service vehicle.

Hot starts – Common starting malfunction of jet engines—the inner temperature is rising too fast and threatens to exceed limits.

Hung starts – Common starting malfunction of jet engines—the engine rotation speed fails to accelerate up to the normal RPM.

ILS – Instrument Landing System – A system of electronic signals, lights and runway markings that permit an aircraft to land in reduced visibility.

Instrument Rating / Instrument Flying / Instrument Pilot – Pilots qualified to fly the aircraft and navigate in the instrument system, beyond visual references.

Intersection takeoff / Departure – An intersection along the length of a runway where an aircraft can gain access to the runway when they don't need its full length.

Lift – Lift is the force that directly opposes the weight of an airplane and holds the airplane in the air. Most of the lift on a normal airliner is generated by the wings.

Line Flying, Lines, Blocks – Flight crews' schedules are assigned month-by-month, through a seniority-based bidding system. A month's schedule of flights is referred to as a 'line' or 'block.'

Line Pilot – A pilot who routinely carries out the airline's core business of transporting passengers and/or cargo.

Link Trainer – An early predecessor to a flight simulator.

Mark One Human Eyeball – When pilots look out the window and make decisions based on visual references, i.e. The hard-to-improve upon human eyeball.

MEL – Minimum Equipment List – A list of aircraft systems or components that are allowed to be unserviceable under specific conditions.

MDA – Minimum Descent Altitude.

NDB (Non-directional Beacon) – Radio beacons located at strategic navigation points.

New-Hire Pilots – The "newbies," "trainees," or "new kids on the block."

"No Go" point – A point we will not pass without making a conscious decision to turn back or continue.

Pairings – A set of flights that begin and end at a pilot's domicile or home base.

Paper Tiger – A full-sized paper or wooden mock-up of the aircraft instrument panels. Once basic functions are mastered, the student pilot will progress on to simulators. AKA "Procedures Trainer."

PIC – Pilot In Command.

PIOs – Pilot Induced Oscillations.

Pilot's Favorite Remedy – A humorous reference to the fact that sometimes a bump, a thump or recycling a key piece of equipment can make problems go away.

PF (The Pilot Flying) – Pilot responsible for manipulating the flight controls and maneuvering and navigating the aircraft.

PIREPS – Pilot reports.

Pitch – Rotational movement of the aircraft around its lateral (side-to-side) axis (see Roll and Yaw).

PM (The Pilot Monitoring) – Pilot responsible for double-checking all critical actions of the PF, making audible challenges to ensure the PF is aware of speeds and altitudes.

PP – Problematic Passenger. Author's unofficial terminology.

Purser — The "in-charge" flight attendant is the cabin manager who is responsible for passenger safety and service procedures.

QRH (Quick Reference Handbook) – A booklet where pilots can quickly find checklists needed regularly or especially in an emergency.

Radio Altimeter – An electronic gauge that uses radar to measure altitude

Ragwing Fleet Canucks – A type of small, two-place aircraft used by many Canadian flying clubs and schools after WWII. Ragwing refers to their fabric-covered construction.

Ramp (tarmac) – The paved area of an airport aside from runways and taxiways used by an aircraft. It usually includes all the parking areas around gates and hangars.

Ramp Agent / Lead Agent – The person in charge of aircraft servicing while at the gate.

Recency Rules – Regulatory requirements for a pilot to be considered current.

Roll – Rotational movement of the aircraft around its longitudinal (front to back) axis (see Pitch and Yaw).

Roll-out – The part of the landing after the wheels are firmly on the ground until the aircraft slows to taxi speed.

RTO – Rejected takeoff.

Second Officer (SO) – Third flight crew member on aircraft requiring it (rare now).

SBUs / Silicon-based units – Tongue-in-cheek expression for computers, especially those used in automated flight control systems.

Sim Sessions – Flight simulator sessions.

Sky-Caps – Personnel available to help passengers with their luggage. Some airports provide a drive-through luggage check-in service, for example.

SM – Statute mile (vis-à-vis nautical mile).

SOPs (Standard Operating Procedures) – The tightly-scripted methods used to operate the aircraft.

Tarmac – See Ramp.

Thrust, Thrusters / Thrust Levers / Reverse / Reversers – A system of valves and internal components that blocks a jet engine's normal exhaust pathway while redirecting a percentage of thrust in the opposite direction, producing a decelerating force.

Transmissometers – Devices that detect the visibility along specific runways.

Turn Final – The last turn to intercept the final approach track (see Final Approach Track).

Uplift – The action of transferring fuel from a truck or hydrant into an aircraft.

Vector – The direction an airplane flies.

Vectored / vectoring – A navigation service provided to pilots by air traffic controllers, guiding an airplane to the desired point.

Vertical Detents – When selecting reverse thrust, a mechanical interlock mechanism, or detent, prevents the levers from moving further rearwards until the inner mechanisms of the engines have finished adjusting.

V speeds – A set of defined, critical speeds, which are calculated for every takeoff, to ensure the aircraft is operated as safely as possible, while uplifting the most payload.

V1 (Vee One) – The maximum speed at which the takeoff may be discontinued, and the aircraft stopped within the remaining runway distance.

V2 (Vee Two) – The target speed for the initial climb-out.

Vr (Vee Ar) – Rotation speed. The point where the pilot begins raising the nose of the aircraft to initiate the lift-off.

Wind-shear – A sudden change in wind speed or direction that can pose a danger to aircraft during takeoffs or landings.

Yaw – Rotational movement of the aircraft around its vertical axis (see Pitch and Roll).

Acknowledgements

✈   ✈   ✈

Thanks to CWRpress and especially to Greg Albrecht for the opportunity and encouragement, without which this project could never have happened.

Thanks to Brad Jersak and Laura Urista for their guidance and dedication to the editing process and to Dennis Warkentin who handles promotion and so much more.

Special thanks to all the crew members and colleagues who lived these stories with me.

Also by GRANT CORRIVEAU

✈   ✈   ✈

Airline Pilot: A Day in the Life – Join an experienced A320 flight crew as they face a typical day's work "on the line." From the hectic pace of irregular operations, turbulence and quick turn-arounds to landing in marginal weather with minimal fuel reserves, this detailed description of a line pilot's job places you in the heart of the action. Available soon on Kindle.

Printed in Great Britain
by Amazon

19809667R00122